201 Organic Baby AND Toddler Meals

The Healthiest Toddler and Baby Food Recipes You Can Make!

TAMIKA L. GARDNER, author of *201 Organic Baby Purées*

adamsmedia

AVON, MASSACHUSETTS

Published by
Adams Media, a division of F+W Media, Inc.
57 Littlefield Street, Avon, MA 02322. U.S.A.
www.adamsmedia.com

Contains material adapted and abridged from *The Everything® Busy Moms' Cookbook* by Susan Whetzel, copyright © 2013 by F+W Media, Inc., ISBN 10: 1-4405-5925-2, ISBN 13: 978-1-4405-5925-9; *The Everything® Cooking for Kids Cookbook* by Ronni Litz Julien, copyright © 2010 by F+W Media, Inc., ISBN 10: 1-60550-665-6, ISBN 13: 978-1-60550-665-4; and *The Everything® Organic Cooking for Baby and Toddler Book* by Kim Lutz and Megan Hart, MS, RD, copyright © 2008 by F+W Media, Inc., ISBN 10: 1-59869-926-1, ISBN 13: 978-1-59869-926-5.

ISBN 10: 1-4405-8161-4
ISBN 13: 978-1-4405-8161-8
eISBN 10: 1-4405-8162-2
eISBN 13: 978-1-4405-8162-5

Printed in the United States of America.

10 9 8 7 6 5 4 3 2 1

Library of Congress Cataloging-in-Publication Data

Gardner, Tamika L.
  201 organic baby and toddler meals / Tamika L. Gardner
    pages cm
  Includes index.
  ISBN 978-1-4405-8161-8 (pb) -- ISBN 1-4405-8161-4 (pb) -- ISBN
978-1-4405-8162-5 (ebook) -- ISBN 1-4405-8162-2 (ebook)
1. Baby foods. 2. Infants--Nutrition. 3. Toddlers--Nutrition.
4. Cooking (Natural foods) I. Title. II. Title: Two hundred and one
organic baby and toddler meals. III. Title: Two hundred-one organic
baby and toddler meals.
  RJ216.G26 2014
  641.3'02--dc23
                        2014028825

Many of the designations used by manufacturers and sellers to distinguish their products are claimed as trademarks. Where those designations appear in this book and F+W Media, Inc. was aware of a trademark claim, the designations have been printed with initial capital letters.

Always follow safety and commonsense cooking protocol while using kitchen utensils, operating ovens and stoves, and handling uncooked food. If children are assisting in the preparation of any recipe, they should always be supervised by an adult.

This book is intended as general information only and should not be used to diagnose or treat any health condition. In light of the complex, individual, and specific nature of health problems, this book is not intended to replace professional medical advice. The ideas, procedures, and suggestions in this book are intended to supplement, not replace, the advice of a trained medical professional. Consult your physician before adopting any of the suggestions in this book, as well as about any condition that may require diagnosis or medical attention. The author and publisher disclaim any liability arising directly or indirectly from the use of this book.

Photos by Jennifer Yandle Photography (*www.jenniferyandle.com*). Cover design and photography by Erin Dawson.

This book is available at quantity discounts for bulk purchases. For information, please call 1-800-289-0963.

DEDICATION

This book is dedicated to my loving family,
Troy, Nikai, and Troy II

-and-

To my grandparents,
Catherine Eggleston, and Joe and Arrie McCullar.

CONTENTS

CHAPTER 7: The Independent Toddler—2 to 3 Years...189

ORGANIC AWARENESS

It's amazing how children can change your life. Even though I considered myself a fairly healthy person, I was not an ingredient scrutinizer like I am now. I realized that the food I *thought* was healthy was actually laden with flavor-enhancing chemicals, pesticides, and consisted of a laundry list of ingredients I couldn't pronounce.

You can see the effects of unhealthy eating all around you on a daily basis. According to the Centers for Disease Control and Prevention (CDC), approximately 12.5 million children and adolescents are obese. It's no wonder, when processed food has been the primary source of consumption for decades.

When I found out I was going to be a new mother, I immediately headed online to research foods that I should eat to provide optimum nutrition for my unborn child. I learned how to read the ingredients on packaging and figured out which ingredients to steer clear from. Eventually, more and more items I used to buy disappeared from my kitchen. My husband would ask me, "Honey, didn't you go grocery shopping today? Where is all the food?" I told him how the snacks and prepared foods he loved had so many unhealthy ingredients I couldn't bring myself to use those items in our home anymore. He totally supported my new approach, and the mental shift we made changed us for the better—forever. Surprisingly for me, I realized I had a lot more money to spend on healthier items because I wasn't purchasing the more expensive prepackaged, processed items. It was time to learn how to make *real* food for my family—from scratch, with *real* ingredients—and it started with making homemade baby food.

After our daughter was born in 2006, I wanted her to have the best nutrition that money could *not* buy. So, I produced my own milk via breastfeeding and made her baby food with some of the ingredients I grew in my own small garden. After our son came along 18 months later, I became a pro at making baby food and I had three organic vegetable beds right outside my doorstep. I didn't know a whole lot about the adverse affects of pesticide use at that time, but my natural instincts would not allow me to buy chemicals to spray my plants that I would later harvest and give to my babies. Back online I went, researching natural ways to deter insects from eating at my collards and tomatoes without using chemical products.

I found that making homemade meals wasn't as expensive or difficult as I feared. By planning ahead, using local ingredients, and finding uses for leftovers, I was able to make most of our family's meals (my husband also chipped in). You can do it, too!

As my infants became toddlers, I was faced with a new challenge of offering them new, interesting dishes and coming up with organic meals and substitutes for items that I could not find in organic (or that were too expensive). Toddlers can eat more of a variety of foods than infants—but they can also be pickier eaters. In this book, you'll find delicious, healthy recipes that you can make using whole ingredients, including organic, homemade versions of popular store-bought items such as salad dressing, toaster pastries, bread crumbs, and sauces. Your toddler will love eating the meals, and you'll love serving them.

I won't have you spending time making funny faces and dinosaur shapes with food. However, I will show you how to make good meals with ingredients you can actually find, and feel good about feeding to your family.

Cheers to raising a healthy eater!

[signature]

EMBRACE HOME-COOKED FOOD

The time has come for parents to get back in the kitchen and start cooking for their families again. Now that your infant has graduated from my first book, *201 Organic Baby Purées*, here are 201 more organic meals that you can make for your child from 9 months to 3 years old. Being an active chef in your household means that you get to make healthy decisions and use the ingredients you feel are the most nutritious for your children. Gone are the days when you could blindly buy processed or chemical-rich foods. Now we know the benefits of whole foods to give your children the nourishment they need for healthy brain development and strong immune systems.

Today, organics are everywhere, and there are more organic farmers than ever before. You don't have to drive 30 miles one way to reach the only health food store in town anymore. Now you can walk to your favorite farm stand on the corner, or take a short drive to a farmers' market or national grocery chain, where you'll find a variety of organic foods.

Stocking your kitchen with organic fruit, vegetables, and lean meat means your family has a lower risk of exposure to pesticides and other harmful chemicals that are found in conventional and processed foods. When you stock your kitchen with natural, whole ingredients, you can create an endless number of delicious, healthy recipes. The recipes in this book include a larger assortment of fruit and vegetable recipes to encourage children, at a young age, to eat more produce.

When you embrace cooking family meals, you will see it is not as hard as you thought and you might even get your creative juices flowing and come up with healthy family recipes that can be passed down for generations. As you create the recipes in this book, you will connect more with food. Even though it's easy enough to spend a few dollars on a bottle of honey mustard dressing and call it a day, you will gain new insights from making your own honey mustard dressing and you will start to look at all packaged foods differently. These recipes are all easy to make, and will appeal to everyone in your family— toddler or not. Even though toddlers can be picky, their palates are also a blank slate. Offer them a variety of textures, flavors, and consistencies, and see which they prefer. In this book, you'll find simple but sophisticated dishes, from Chilled White Grape Peach Soup (Chapter 4) to Fruit-Infused Milk (Chapter 5) to Magic Mango Coleslaw (Chapter 6) to Cilantro Lime Jasmine Rice (Chapter 6). The toughest part will be deciding which recipe to try first!

QUICK REFERENCE GUIDE FOR RECIPES

Making meals from scratch can seem like a daunting task, especially if you feel like there is not enough time in the day to accomplish everything. Just like with baby purées, many of the meals in this book can be made in larger quantities, frozen, or made in advance on days when you have more time to spare than others. The following icons will help you quickly identify recipes that might appeal to you and your family:

 Freezer-Friendly—These recipes can be safely frozen for up to 2 weeks for the best quality.

 On-the-Go—These recipes are great to pack and take on the go.

 Gluten-Free—These recipes do not contain gluten. Children with gluten intolerance or gluten sensitivity are not able to eat foods that contain gluten, including some types of pastas, bread, and any form of wheat, rye, oats (unless labeled "gluten-free"), and barley. Although lots of foods contain these ingredients, you can now find many gluten-free organic products on the market. Also, lean meat, fruit, veggies, legumes, and many dairy products are naturally gluten-free. Consult with your healthcare provider to determine your child's specific dietary needs.

 Toxic Twenty—This icon is listed next to recipe ingredients that are high in pesticides and should be purchased organic if possible.

PART 1

READY, SET, PREP

When thinking about organic meals, begin with your goal in mind: Ultimately, you want to raise a child who prefers a beautiful green leafy salad with a bowl of fresh fruit and yogurt rather than one who only prefers cupcakes and potato chips. And, you want to ensure that your child is getting a good amount of antioxidants (to help fight illness and disease), nutrients, and fats needed to support healthy development and growth. In this section, you will learn about organic food production, why choosing organic foods is important, and how to stock your kitchen so that you can make the recipes in this book and get creative in the kitchen with your little one.

CHAPTER 1

ORGANICS BOOT CAMP
WHY ORGANIC FOODS ARE HEALTHIER FOR YOUR CHILD

WHAT MAKES FOOD ORGANIC?

Organic food is produced by farmers who rely on naturally occurring living organisms and other environmental factors to reduce the risks of pests and diseases in plants and animals. These natural methods encourage a healthier environment for all living things.

Organic foods are free from harmful pesticides, sewage sludge, hormones, genetic modification, artificial fertilizers, and antibiotics. The United States Department of Agriculture (USDA) oversees the National Organic Program, which certifies organic producers to ensure that agriculture is produced using renewable resources and methods that sustain soil and water and protect the environment. Organic growers are inspected yearly to assure compliance with these regulations.

A BRIEF HISTORY OF ORGANIC FARMING

Farming methods had been organic up until the World War II era, when chemicals were introduced to eliminate insects that sometimes ravaged food supplies. A Swiss chemist named Paul Müller discovered the insecticidal action of a chemical compound known as DDT, which was used by the U.S. military during the war to fight off disease-carrying insects. After the war, farmers adopted the use of DDT on commercial farms, not yet knowing its hazardous effects to humans and the environment.

In 1972, the United States banned the agricultural use of DDT, after research showed its ill effects on humans and the environment. Farmers then turned to other types of chemicals to reduce insect infestations. In the last decade organic farming has become widespread and the preferred choice of many parents.

HOW TO TELL IF IT'S REALLY ORGANIC

If a product is really organic, you will see a seal that says "USDA Organic" imprinted on the product packaging, or as a sticker applied to items like fresh produce. The seal indicates that the product is certified and has at least 95 percent organic content. When you see the seal, it's the real deal.

Many products on the market today proclaim themselves "all-natural" or "free-range," but those terms do not mean the food was produced using organic methods. Unless you see the certified organic seal from the USDA, the product is not organic.

Here are some of the common claims you may see on labels or product packaging, and what they really mean. The USDA verifies the following claims are accurate and truthful:

- **Natural**—This claim is regulated by the USDA only when applied to meat and poultry. Meat, poultry, and eggs must be minimally processed and contain no artificial ingredients, including flavors, colors, or preservatives, in order to use this claim. *"Natural" claims on food products other than meat, poultry, or eggs are not regulated by the USDA.* You'll see this word used all the time on foods that are not organic—and not even good for you—such as potato chips and cookies.
- **Free-Range**—This claim is regulated by the USDA and only applies to poultry. "Free-range" means that the flock is given unrestricted space and can wander freely indoors and outdoors with unlimited access to food and water.

- **Cage-Free**—Regulated by the USDA, this claim applies to laying hens and means that they are able to wander freely, but within an enclosed area, with unlimited access to fresh food and water. The hens may or may not have access to the outdoors.
- **No Hormones Added** or **Raised Without Hormones**—All food companies are able to make this claim because federal regulations have never permitted hormones or steroids in poultry, pork, or goat.
- **Grass-Fed**—This claim is regulated by the USDA and means that the animals feed on grass throughout their life. However, current regulations don't limit the use of antibiotics, hormones, or pesticides that the animals are exposed to.
- **Vegetarian-Fed**—This claim isn't regulated by the USDA. It implies that animals are fed a healthier diet, without animal byproducts or dairy products.

ORGANIC FOODS ARE HEALTHIER FOR CHILDREN

There has been much debate over whether or not organic produce is superior to conventionally grown foods in terms of nutrition and health benefits for both adults and children. According to the American Academy of Pediatrics (AAP), both organic and conventionally grown foods have the same nutrient content that are vital to a child's health. Some studies show that organic foods have higher nutritional content in terms of vitamins and minerals, but not enough to make an impact on overall health. However, when it comes to health advantages, the AAP clearly states, "Organic diets have been convincingly demonstrated to expose consumers to fewer pesticides associated with human disease."

Pesticide exposure in infants and children can pose serious health risks. According to the United States Environmental Protection Agency (EPA), children are not only exposed to pesticides from foods, but also at school, on playgrounds, around the home, and from their own parents' clothing (if their parents work in agriculture). Children's bodies are developing and maturing, and they do not process toxins the same way that adults do.

Choosing organic foods and eliminating toxic chemicals in your home and garden is a great first step to limiting your child's pesticide exposure. While it's impossible to protect your children from everything, the good news is that you can certainly make an impact through the things you have direct control over.

THE ENVIRONMENTAL BENEFITS OF ORGANIC FOODS

By purchasing organic food, you support a healthier world. Why? Organic farming practices consider environmental impact. While conventional farming can pollute the environment with chemical fertilizers, synthetic insecticides, and herbicides, organic farming does not. Instead, organic farming relies on natural sources to promote healthy soil, plants, and animals. This includes utilizing creatures that are already a part of nature, such as beneficial insects to help reduce diseases and pests. For example, instead of using chemicals, organic farmers may use beneficial nematodes to prevent weevil infestations that can ruin plant tissue in carrots, celery, parsnips, and parsley.

All creatures have a role in the circle of life. For example, plants need honeybees for pollination and humans rely on fruit and vegetables to live. Without bees, the majority of fruit and vegetables would disappear, causing devastating effects to life as we know it. Because organic foods are raised in harmony with nature, there are no threats of pollution, decline in species due to pesticide poisoning, or potential health defects in children. It is truly a win-win for everyone.

TOP FOODS TO PURCHASE ORGANIC: THE TOXIC TWENTY

Although the goal is to reduce pesticide exposure and support environmentally friendly farming practices, giving your child nonorganic produce is better than not offering it at all, or resorting to processed alternatives. But when purchasing organics is not financially feasible, consider the pesticide load (the amount of pesticides found in produce) before making a purchase. According to the Environmental Working Group (EWG), apples, strawberries, and grapes carry the most pesticides (and are called "dirty"), so those foods should always be purchased organic. However, foods like sweet corn and avocados are safer to purchase nonorganic because they are usually exposed to a lower amount of pesticides (and are called "clean").

Therefore, you want to purchase foods that have the lowest amount of pesticides, according to the research of the EWG. The following is a list of the top twenty foods that you should always buy organic because of their pesticide load. To help you remember, these ingredients are **bolded** in the recipes that follow (lower numbers equal more pesticides):

THE TOXIC TWENTY

1. Apples
2. Strawberries
3. Grapes
4. Celery
5. Peaches
6. Spinach
7. Sweet bell peppers
8. Nectarines (imported)
9. Cucumbers
10. Cherry tomatoes
11. Snap peas (imported)
12. Potatoes
13. Hot peppers
14. Blueberries (domestic)
15. Lettuce
16. Kale/collard greens
17. Plums
18. Cherries
19. Nectarines (domestic)
20. Pears

To download the most up-to-date "clean and dirty" list, go to *www.foodnews.org*.

CHAPTER 2

MEAL PLANNING AND PREPARATION
TIPS TO MAKE FAMILY MEALS STRESS-FREE

SET A GOOD EXAMPLE

Now that you have a baby who is paying attention to everything you do, it's time to evaluate your eating and shopping habits. You don't necessarily have to restrict what you purchase or become extra rigid and controlled about what you eat, but you certainly want to set a good, yet balanced, example. Your toddler is very impressionable, so make a good impression while the window of opportunity is open.

When figuring out what to prepare for your family, a little time spent planning up front can save valuable time later. One of the hardest and time-consuming chores is figuring out what to make (on the fly) on a daily basis. Not having all the ingredients you need to make the meal you thought about will only make matters worse. To avoid the dinnertime panic, set aside a small amount of time each week or month and write out the meals you plan to make. Once you assemble a couple of months' worth of meals, recycle the plans and shopping lists and use them again. Following are a few other things to keep in mind as you think about mealtimes.

PLAN ON FAMILY TIME AT THE TABLE

In a country where almost everyone (even the 2-year-olds) in the household has a hand-held electronic device and there's a television in every room, it is now more important than ever before to sit down and have a family meal, free of electronic devices and other distractions, at least once a day. Even better, each time *anyone* in your household sits down for a meal, give the electronics a break. No more scooting the baby's highchair in front of the TV so you can get laundry done while she eats. Not only does that behavior promote unhealthy eating habits that can spill over into adulthood, but it also can condition your child to *not* eat unless the tube is on.

Studies have shown that eating family meals encourages healthier eating habits, and it's also a time to connect and bond. Use this time to talk to your spouse or significant other about the benefits of eating healthy in front of your child. Bring up positive topics related to food. While your toddler is eating she is also listening, so take advantage of the time by sending the right messages. By the time she is 6 years old, she'll have absorbed messages like:

- Fruit and vegetables are healthy fuels for your body.
- A healthy diet can help prevent illnesses.
- Exercise complements a healthy diet to promote overall well-being.

You may even hear your son or daughter repeating these same messages to others—or reminding you if you slip up!

OFFER A VARIETY OF FOODS

It is important to offer your child a variety of fresh fruit, vegetables, and lean protein to make sure her nutritional needs are being met, and also to encourage an adventurous eater. The more variety you introduce at a young age, the better.

However, it is equally important to be very thoughtful and deliberate about *how much* variety you will offer in a given week so that you aren't throwing away a lot of uneaten food. Cook your family favorites most days of the week, and introduce one or two new, well-balanced meals per week, choosing recipes that are based on ingredients you have on hand. Organic foods can cost slightly more, so make sure the food you purchase can be used to make multiple recipes or be frozen for future use.

TYPES OF FAT

You already know to include plenty of fruit and veggies in your child's meals, along with healthy sources of proteins. But many people misunderstand the importance of fats in a toddler's diet. Fat plays an integral part of your children's diet and should be incorporated into meals to help fuel their rapid growth. Breast milk and infant formula both contain lots of fat and up until 12 months it is their primary fat source. According to the American Academy of Pediatrics, babies and toddlers under age two should obtain about 50 percent of their total energy (calories) from fat and gradually reduce the amount at the age of two so it's down to about one-third by age four or five. As you meal-plan, be sure to account for the healthy fats your growing toddler needs.

Here are the basic types of fats:

- **Unsaturated fats** are commonly found in plant-based oils and fish. There are two types of unsaturated fats:

  - *Monounsaturated fat*—found in avocados, nuts, and vegetable oils including olive, canola, and peanut oil. Studies show that consuming monounsaturated fats can lower bad cholesterol levels.
  - *Polyunsaturated fat*—found in vegetable oils such as sunflower, sesame, soybean, and corn oils, as well as seafood. Omega-3 and omega-6 essential fatty acids are types of polyunsaturated fat essential for brain and visual development. We

currently consume a lot more omega-6 fats since those fats are included in sunflower, safflower, and corn oil. However, the American Heart Association recommends focusing on getting more omega-3 fats from sources such as salmon, tuna, flaxseed, canola oil, kale, eggs, and tofu.

- **Saturated fat** is found mostly in animal products, including milk, cheese, and meat, as well as in coconut oil, palm oil, and cocoa butter. This type of fat is known for increasing blood cholesterol levels and the risk of heart disease in adults when consumed in large amounts over the course of life. Yet the American Academy of Pediatrics notes that cholesterol and other fats are very important for babies and therefore should not be restricted.
- **Trans fats** are commonly found in margarine and many processed foods, including snacks and baked goods. Trans fats are created through an industrial process called hydrogenation. This process adds hydrogen to vegetable oils to make them more solid. Trans fats are associated with raising bad cholesterol levels, lowering good cholesterol levels, and increasing the risk for developing type 2 diabetes, heart disease, and stroke—so you want to stay away from eating too much of this type. Look at the ingredients list on the food label for "partially hydrogenated oils" to spot trans fat or on the nutrition facts panel and limit your toddler's intake accordingly.

KEEPING TRACK OF THE WINNERS AND THE LOSERS

One thing I've found helpful is keeping a list, or at least a mental note, of the foods your toddler loves (the winners) and a list of the ones he didn't care for as much (the losers). This is especially helpful while he is young so that you can try preparing the losers in a different way. As your child gets older, the wide range of foods he had no problem eating as a young toddler can narrow to some degree. This is a phase—though a seemingly very long phase—that your child may go through, but rest assured it has absolutely nothing to do with you. The key is to *consistently* offer meals including whole grains, fruit, vegetables, protein, and healthy fats so that your child knows what a healthy meal looks like. Serve foods you know your toddler will eat, but don't be afraid to keep trying options he didn't like. He'll eventually learn to keep trying the disliked foods, especially if he's hungry enough! I know it may seem out of the question, but it can take about twenty times to acquire a taste for something, so don't rule out anything just yet.

It is not necessary to make a separate meal for your toddler when you're also cooking for the rest of the family. Older children and adults may find the recipes in this book delicious as well, so feel free to double or triple the ingredients to make enough for everyone.

TIPS FOR SMART SHOPPING

There's no way around it: Shopping for organics can be costly. However, you can save money with these easy tips:

- **Always buy in-season produce.** Produce is more expensive when it is out of season. Stock up during the growing season and freeze for later so you can enjoy the food year round at a more reasonable cost. Visit *www.fruitsandveggiesmorematters .org* for a list of when certain fruit and vegetables are in season.
- **Watch for sales.** Many stores offer sales on organic produce, as they would any other product. Check their weekly ad or sign up to receive offers via e-mail or smartphone.
- **Buy in bulk.** Bulk prices are a great way to get a lot of one item for a low price. If you won't eat the whole quantity before it spoils, you can freeze, can, or share it with a neighbor or family member.

- **Buy generic organic brands.** As long as you see the USDA seal on packaging, it doesn't matter what brand you choose. Stores like Kroger, Whole Foods, and Costco carry their own organic brands and they are just as good as the rest. Many store brands also offer a 200 percent guarantee on produce, so if the food you bought doesn't live up to your expectations, cruise right back into the store for an exchange and your money back too! Each store varies, so check its policy before you go.
- **Save those coupons.** Anytime you get a coupon for organic produce, be it fresh or frozen, clip it or save it on your smartphone, and use it before it expires. Some stores require a coupon in order to get the sale price, so clip, clip, clip!

TEN GREAT PLACES TO BUY ORGANICS

You probably have several places nearby where you can buy organic foods. Here are some traditional outlets, as well as chain options:

1. Farmers' markets
2. "Pick your own" farms
3. Community Supported Agriculture (CSA)
4. Whole Foods
5. Earth Fare
6. Harris Teeter
7. Trader Joe's
8. Costco
9. BJ's Wholesale Club
10. Walmart

CONSIDER GROWING YOUR OWN FOOD

If you have space in your backyard, consider growing your own organic produce and save money long-term. It will be a small investment to convert your soil to organic and to purchase necessary materials, but the long-term benefits are rewarding.

Community gardens are also on the rise. For a nominal annual fee, you can bring home whatever produce you like in exchange for a little labor each week. Check out the American Community Gardening Association at *www.communitygarden.org* to find a garden near you.

CHAPTER 3

KITCHEN AND PANTRY ESSENTIALS
EVERYDAY ITEMS TO HAVE ON HAND

STOCKING YOUR KITCHEN WITH THE ESSENTIALS

You'll only need a few everyday kitchen items to make cooking organic foods a stress-free and enjoyable experience. Some of these will help reduce the time you spend in the kitchen so you can have more time with your family.

Here are a few kitchen tools that I recommend you use for quick meal preparation:

- **Full-size food processor.** This tool is invaluable for chopping, slicing, and grating fruit and vegetables. This is my preferred tool for making chopped salad, salad dressings, and salsas quickly.
- **Sharp knives.** Make sure you have an assortment of sharp knives on hand for precise cutting. Dull knives waste time and cause frustration.
- **Cutting boards.** You'll need one cutting board for cutting meats and another for cutting produce. Choose two different colors or styles to be able to differentiate between the two. This will help reduce the risk of cross-contamination. Make sure both are dishwasher safe and eco-friendly.
- **Salad spinner.** This is handy for drying produce quickly and effectively without using up paper or kitchen towels—saving water and trees.
- **Blender.** This tool can blend liquid ingredients and is perfect for making smoothies and popsicles.

- **Freezable glass containers.** You will need a few of these to freeze meals prepared ahead of time. Glass containers will help save money because they are reusable and last a lifetime. Plus, they don't retain flavors and smells like plastic containers can.
- **Nonstick cookware.** A variety of options, such as pots, pans, skillets, baking sheets, and muffin pans, are everyday essentials.
- **Silpat liners.** More economical than parchment paper, these liners help prevent your baked foods from burning on the bottom, and they make cleanup a snap. These liners are helpful to have but are not essential.
- **Ice pop molds.** Any style mold will work, so choose a few you think your child will adore. These will be helpful for making the ice pop recipes in this book.
- **Grater.** This tool is a lifesaver for grating cheese and carrots if you don't have a food processor.
- **Measuring utensils.** Liquid and dry measuring cups and spoons are a must-have to ensure that your recipes turn out successfully. Having more than one set of measuring spoons is also a good idea so you can eliminate time spent on washing in between measuring ingredients.
- **Spatulas and spoons.** Silicone spatulas and wooden spoons will help scrape and stir ingredients.
- **A pair of tongs.** Tongs are excellent for picking up food and to keep fingers from getting burned. They can also prevent cross-contamination—use a clean pair of tongs to move cooked meat, instead of the utensil you used to touch the uncooked meat, for example.
- **Meat thermometer.** A meat thermometer is an absolute must to ensure your meats are cooked thoroughly to avoid the risk of illness.
- **Flip waffle iron.** A good nonstick waffle iron with at least 1" wells is ideal for making perfect Belgian waffles at home for breakfast and snacks.

STAPLES FOR A WELL-STOCKED ORGANIC KITCHEN

When it's time to cook, there is nothing like having everything you need on hand to make meals for your family. Use this list as a guide to keep a well-stocked kitchen full of commonly used ingredients to make a variety of healthy meals in a pinch. All of the ingredients in this list can be purchased organic.

FRESH PRODUCE

- Bananas
- Apples
- Pears
- Sweet potatoes
- Onions
- Broccoli
- Avocados
- Cabbage
- Kale
- Carrots
- Roma tomatoes
- Cucumbers
- Mandarin oranges/clementines
- Celery

SPICES AND EXTRACTS

- Cinnamon
- Nutmeg
- Thyme
- Dill
- Paprika (smoked works best)
- Garlic powder
- Ginger
- Kosher salt
- Pepper
- Pure vanilla extract

HERBS

- Mint
- Parsley
- Oregano
- Bay leaves (dried)

- Dill
- Thyme
- Cilantro

OILS

- Extra-virgin olive oil
- Extra-virgin coconut oil

- Canola oil
- Grape seed oil

DAIRY PRODUCTS AND NONDAIRY SUBSTITUTES

- Eggs (choose medium or large organic eggs)
- Cheese (mild Cheddar, mozzarella, Parmesan, and cream cheese)
- Yogurt (look for full-fat yogurt for toddlers under 2 years old)
- Unsalted butter
- Milk (whole cow's milk, goat's milk, coconut, enriched soy, or rice milk)
- Tofu

STAPLE PRODUCTS

- Chicken and vegetable stock (low-sodium varieties or homemade)
- Pasta (mini spaghetti, farfalle, rotini, shells, or pasta stars)
- Rice (Arborio rice, wild rice, white and brown long grain)

- Beans and legumes (garbanzo beans, lima beans, black-eyed peas, pinto beans, and black beans)
- Cereals (rolled oats, grits, granola, and muesli)
- Flour (unbleached all-purpose and whole wheat)
- Whole-grain breads

You probably have many of these kitchen items and food products on hand already. That means you can dive right into making these yummy recipes.

PART 2

THE RECIPES: ORGANIC MEALS FOR GROWING APPETITES

In the following chapters, you'll find 201 amazing, wholesome, organic meals that you can prepare at home. Starting at 9 months, your child can handle chunky and lumpier textures, so you don't need to exclusively blend purées from this point forward. This is an exciting moment, when you can take your baby out on the town to purchase new feeding dishes, sippy cups, baby spoons, and forks to celebrate this new stage in her development—eating solid foods!

This part includes recipes for the following age groups:

The Transitioner—9 to 12 months

The Explorer—12 to 18 months

The Picky Eater—18 to 24 months

The Independent Toddler—2 to 3 years

CHAPTER 4
THE TRANSITIONER—
9 TO 12 MONTHS

As you transition your child to solid foods, he will experience new foods and flavors and will be excited to investigate (and smush . . . and throw) every green pea or carrot that you put on his plate. At this time, he may be more inclined to use his fingers as eating utensils, so things could get a little messy. Prepare for this transition by keeping plenty of bibs on hand and making sure your toddler isn't dressed in his Sunday's best at mealtimes. Allow him to have time to establish a relationship with food, and accept the mess that comes with it. It's a new beginning for both of you.

Although solid foods will increasingly replace breast milk or formula, at this age, milk is still an important source of nutrition. Therefore, make sure your child has 24–32 ounces per day, or 16 ounces of whole cow's milk at 12 months. Limit fruit juice to 2–4 ounces per *day*, not per meal. You may want to dilute certain juices with 50 percent water to prevent tooth decay and a preference for sweet drinks. If you're giving your baby enough whole-fruit servings, whether diced in chunks or blended, fruit juice is not necessary. Instead, introduce small amounts of purified water, especially in hot weather, to set up a foundation of good water-drinking habits later on.

IMPORTANT TIPS TO REMEMBER FOR THE TRANSITIONER

- No honey. Honey is dangerous and can be fatal for babies under 12 months of age.
- Keep finger foods handy, such as toast, crackers, dry cereals, or teething biscuits, for chewing practice and gum soothing.
- Brush any teeth as soon as they come in twice per day with a small smear of natural toothpaste.
- Gradually transition to sippy cups. Ditch the bottle altogether by 12 months old.
- Nuts, unpasteurized cheese, and raw eggs are still off-limits.
- Practice good hand-washing habits by washing your baby's hands before and after meals.

Banana Cinnamon Oatmeal

Oats are extremely inexpensive and versatile. Don't bother purchasing preflavored packs of instant oatmeal when you can make so many different oatmeal flavors using fresh ingredients. You also have more flexibility to create flavor combinations that your child loves.

2 SERVINGS

¼ cup quick-cooking oats

½ cup whole milk, or more as needed

1 teaspoon wheat germ

⅛ teaspoon ground cinnamon

½ banana

1. In a small saucepan, combine the oats, milk, wheat germ, and cinnamon over medium-high heat. Bring to a boil. Stir until thickened.

2. Mash the banana with a fork. Stir the banana into the mixture. Serve immediately.

Love Thy Oats

Not only are oats economical, but they are loaded with soluble fiber, antioxidants, calcium, magnesium, B vitamins, and vitamin E. Oats are famous for maintaining healthy blood sugar levels and lowering bad cholesterol. Keep oats stored in an airtight container in a cool, dry place.

Just Peachy Oatmeal

 T20

This light yet flavorful oatmeal has just the right amount of sweetness to start your toddler's day. Make sure the canned organic peaches are in juice.

2 SERVINGS

¼ cup quick-cooking oats

⅓ cup whole milk, or more as needed

4 canned peach slices, cut into small chunks

1 tablespoon juice from canned peaches

⅛ teaspoon ground cinnamon

In a small saucepan, combine all the ingredients over medium high heat. Bring to a boil. Stir until thickened. Serve immediately.

Seasoned Hard-Boiled Eggs

Super simple and easy, hard-boiled eggs are good option for toddlers who don't like the texture of scrambled eggs. Eggs are rich in protein, vitamin D, and essential amino acids. To save time, you can make a bunch of hard-boiled eggs and refrigerate for up to 2 weeks. Use them as is, or make other recipes in this book such as Super Egg Salad (see the recipe in this chapter) or Baby Cobb Salad (Chapter 7).

2 SERVINGS
....

1 large egg
Pinch of kosher salt
Pinch of ground black pepper
Pinch of dried parsley

1. Carefully place the egg in a small pot and add enough water to cover by a couple inches.

2. Heat on medium-high until boiling, and cook uncovered at a rolling boil for an additional 10 minutes. Remove from heat.

3. Let the egg stand in the hot water for an additional 3–5 minutes. Pour out the water and replace it with cold water to cool down the egg enough for peeling.

4. Peel the egg and cut it in half (refrigerate the other half for later). Sprinkle with salt, pepper, and parsley.

Perfect Pairings
Serve ½ hard-boiled egg with a few banana slices and ½ slice whole-grain toast and your child will have an energy-packed breakfast.

Cinnamon French Toast Sticks

Toddlers love this cute twist on traditional French toast because they can "dunk" them in real maple syrup. You can also use fruit preserves instead if you like. For best results, purchase a whole, unsliced loaf of whole-wheat bread and cut thick slices.

4 SERVINGS

8 slices thick-cut whole-wheat bread

4 large eggs

1 cup whole milk

¼ teaspoon salt

¼ teaspoon ground cinnamon

½ teaspoon pure vanilla extract

2 tablespoons unsalted butter

¼ cup pure maple syrup

1. Cut the bread slices lengthwise into 4 equal pieces.

2. In a small bowl, whisk the eggs with the milk, salt, cinnamon, and vanilla.

3. Heat the butter in a skillet on medium to medium-low.

4. One at a time, dip the bread slices into the egg mixture, coating well. (Only dip as many pieces of bread into the mixture as you are cooking at one time.)

5. Lay the soaked bread pieces in the skillet. Cook on one side for about 2 minutes, until browned; turn over and cook the other side until browned.

6. Divide the syrup evenly in small dipping cups. Serve with the French toast sticks.

Blooming Popovers

The first time I had popovers I thought they were super cool because of their big, abnormal shape. No two are alike! The children think they are fun to eat and have lots of fun playing with the fluffy tops before eating them. Serve them with breakfast, as a snack, or with a salad. They can be enjoyed any time of day.

12 SERVINGS

3 large eggs

1 cup whole milk

1 cup unbleached all-purpose flour

1 tablespoon canola oil

¼ teaspoon salt

1. Preheat oven to 425°F. Spray a 12-cup muffin pan with nonstick baking spray and set aside.

2. Combine all the ingredients in a medium bowl and beat well with a wire whisk until the batter is blended and smooth, about 2 minutes. Fill each well halfway with batter. Bake for 15 minutes (don't open the oven door to check on them), then reduce heat to 325°F. Cook for an additional 10 minutes, or until the popovers are puffed and deep golden brown. Serve immediately.

Blueberry Mango Cereal Mix

Spruce up plain store-bought cereal by adding extra nutrition with dried fruit. You can substitute the dried blueberries and mango with other dried fruit you may already have, like dried apples or bananas. Serve this as a finger snack and as your child gets older, you can serve it in a bowl with milk.

16 SERVINGS

2 cups cinnamon whole-wheat cereal, such as Cascadian Farm Cinnamon Crunch Cereal

2 cups organic puff cereal, such as Gerber Graduates Puffs Cereal Snack

2 cups dried blueberries

¼ cup chopped dried mango pieces

Combine all the ingredients and store in an eco-friendly airtight container.

Mango—a Superfruit

Mango is known for its juicy, sweet flavor, distinctive fragrance, and unique shape. It has many potential health benefits, and carries cancer-fighting antioxidants, beta-carotene, vitamin C, potassium, and fiber. It goes well with many sweet and savory dishes so it's totally universal—try it in smoothies, salads, and breads. Dried mango is also great for take-along snacks and cereals.

Smoky Collard Mash

This is a childhood recipe that my grandmother used to make when I was a toddler. We used the cornbread to soak up all the juice from the collards, also known as "pot liqueur." I still love collards mashed with cornbread, and now my children love it too. Boost the protein by adding diced chicken to the mash. Try incorporating cut-up chicken from Baked Chicken Drumsticks (see the recipe in this chapter).

4 SERVINGS
• • • • • • • • • • • • •

4 heaping cups chopped collard greens, washed

1 tablespoon extra-virgin olive oil

1 small yellow onion, chopped

1 clove garlic, minced

4 cups chicken stock (store-bought or homemade—see the recipe in this chapter)

¼ teaspoon smoked paprika

Kosher salt, to taste

Ground black pepper, to taste

1 Savory Cornbread Pancake (see the recipe in this chapter)

1. Combine all the ingredients except the cornbread pancake in a large pot and cook over medium heat until the collards are tender and bright green, about 20–25 minutes.

2. Add ½ cup cooked collards to a small bowl. Use your fingers to mash the cornbread pancake into the collards until combined. Fluff with a fork. Serve immediately. Refrigerate any leftover collards for up to 3 days.

Savory Cornbread Pancakes

These savory pancakes are wonderful when eaten alone, or with Smoky Collard Mash or Slow Cooker Baby Lima Beans (see recipes in this chapter). This recipe makes a big batch that can be frozen for later, if there are any left!

12 SERVINGS

1 cup unbleached bread flour

1 cup yellow cornmeal

½ teaspoon salt

1 teaspoon baking powder

½ stick unsalted butter

1 cup milk

½ cup cold water

2 tablespoons granulated sugar

3 tablespoons canola oil

1. Combine all ingredients except for the canola oil in a large bowl.

2. Heat the oil in a large skillet over medium-high heat. Use a ¼-cup measurement scoop to ladle batter onto the hot skillet. Cook each pancake until bubbles start to form at the top and the underside is lightly golden. Flip to cook the other side until lightly golden. Transfer cooked pancakes to a plate. Repeat for the remaining batter.

3. Serve warm. Refrigerate for up to 3 days or freeze for up to 2 weeks.

Creamed Spinach

This recipe is a nice choice for babies who don't enjoy raw spinach right away. Many kids like the garlic flavor and creaminess of this recipe, so it's definitely worth a try. It seems like a lot of spinach, but it wilts when it cooks. Spinach is full of iron, which is a mineral your growing toddler needs.

6 SERVINGS

2 teaspoons extra-virgin olive oil

¼ cup chopped yellow onion

2 cloves garlic, minced

6 cups fresh baby spinach

4 ounces cream cheese

⅛ teaspoon salt

Pinch of ground black pepper

Pinch of ground nutmeg (optional)

1. In a nonstick skillet, heat the oil on medium. Add the onion and sauté until translucent.

2. Stir in the garlic and spinach. Cook for about 3 minutes, until the spinach is just wilted.

3. Reduce heat to low. Add the cream cheese, salt, pepper, and nutmeg, and cook until heated through, about 2 minutes. Serve immediately. Refrigerate leftovers for up to 2 days.

Garlic Sprouts

If you refrigerate your garlic and don't use it up within a certain amount of time, you will see green sprouts growing from it. This doesn't mean that your garlic is growing more cloves; it means that it is going bad. The flavor won't be as pungent and the cloves will actually deteriorate, so it's best to use garlic before you see the sprouts. For maximum freshness, store your garlic in a cool, dry, and dark place.

Sweet Potato Casserole

When my kids were infants, they loved puréed sweet potatoes. Now that they are older, they still can't get enough and actually prefer them over white potatoes (and I'm happy about that, because they're better for you!). Sweet potatoes are good by themselves, but dress them up with cinnamon, oats, and maple syrup and you've really got a winner.

12 SERVINGS

4 large sweet potatoes, peeled and quartered

⅔ cup whole milk

2 teaspoons ground cinnamon, divided

½ teaspoon ground nutmeg

1 cup rolled oats

¼ cup pure maple syrup

1. Preheat oven to 400°F. Spray the bottom of a 9" x 9" casserole dish with nonstick cooking spray.

2. Place the potatoes in the prepared dish, cover, and bake until fork-tender, about 40 minutes.

3. Mash the potatoes with the milk, 1 teaspoon cinnamon, and nutmeg in the casserole dish. Smooth into an even layer with the back of a spoon.

4. In a small bowl, toss the remaining cinnamon with the oats. Stir in the maple syrup. Spread evenly over the potatoes.

5. Bake on the top oven rack for an additional 30 minutes, or until the topping appears brown and crispy.

Make Your Own Nonstick Spray

You can purchase an oil sprayer at many department stores or kitchen supply stores. You simply fill the oil can with any oil of your choice, such as canola or olive oil (and even lemon juice), give it a few pumps for the pressure to build up, and spray your pans. You'll save money from purchasing nonstick spray cans by making your own with oil on hand.

Baby Shawarma

T20

Shawarma is a Middle Eastern dish traditionally made by roasting meat on a spit for several hours. The meat is then shaved off and rolled up in pita or flatbread with hummus or tahini. This is a deconstructed version of chicken shawarma prepared with a cucumber dill sauce instead of hummus or tahini.

2 SERVINGS

¼ cup plain Greek yogurt

1 tablespoon lemon juice

¼ teaspoon dried parsley
or 1 tablespoon chopped
fresh flat-leaf parsley

2 cloves garlic, minced

½ teaspoon salt

¼ teaspoon ground allspice

¼ teaspoon ground cinnamon

1 large boneless, skinless chicken
breast, cut into small cubes

1 whole-wheat pita bread

CUCUMBER DILL SAUCE

½ cup plain Greek yogurt

**¼ cup peeled and
chopped cucumber**

⅛ teaspoon dried dill

1. In a medium bowl, combine the yogurt, lemon juice, parsley, garlic, salt, allspice, and cinnamon. Add the chicken and toss to coat. Cover and place in the refrigerator to marinate for at least 30 minutes or overnight.

2. Meanwhile, prepare the cucumber sauce by combining the yogurt, cucumber, and dill in a small bowl. Cover and store in the refrigerator.

3. Over medium-high heat, cook the marinated chicken in a large skillet or grill pan until cooked through and no longer pink. Turn heat to low to keep warm.

4. Prepare each serving by combining a portion of the chicken and 1–2 teaspoons of the cucumber sauce. Tear a portion of the pita bread into bite-size pieces and stir them into the chicken mixture. Serve immediately. Refrigerate leftovers for up to 3 days.

Try It with Lamb
Shawarma is also very tasty when prepared with ground lamb, so feel free to substitute if you have lamb on hand.

Baked Chicken Drumsticks

Teething babies love gnawing on chicken drumsticks, so after he's finished eating the meat, give him the drumstick to chew on if your pediatrician approves. Supervised, of course!

12 SERVINGS
....

1 tablespoon extra-virgin olive oil

2 tablespoons apple cider vinegar

2 teaspoons water

½ teaspoon garlic powder

½ teaspoon onion powder

⅛ teaspoon ground black pepper

¼ teaspoon kosher salt

1 teaspoon dried parsley

1 tablespoon unbleached
all-purpose flour

4 chicken drumsticks

1. Mix together all the ingredients except the chicken in an 8" × 8" baking dish. Add the chicken and toss to coat with the marinade. Refrigerate for 30 minutes.

2. Meanwhile, preheat oven to 350°F. Place the baking dish in the oven on the middle rack. Bake for 45 minutes or until a meat thermometer reads 180°F.

3. Remove the skin from the chicken. Cut the meat off the bone (leaving a little meat on the drumstick for later), and cut the meat into small pieces. Serve warm.

Organic Apple Cider Vinegar
Since apple cider vinegar is made from apples, it's important to purchase organic apple cider vinegar to use for cooking and consumption.

Leftover Rotisserie Chicken Stock

Next time you pick up a rotisserie chicken at the market, use the remains to make this savory chicken stock, which you can use in many other recipes in this book. Homemade chicken stock is a lot more flavorful than store-bought, so all your meals will benefit.

APPROXIMATELY 8 CUPS

1 leftover rotisserie chicken carcass
or 1 cooked roast chicken carcass

12 cups cold water, or more as needed

½ yellow onion, chopped

½ red onion, chopped

1 stalk celery, with leafy top, sliced

1 large carrot, peeled and sliced

2 sprigs fresh flat-leaf parsley

1 sprig fresh thyme

1 teaspoon salt

1   Add all the ingredients to a large stockpot over high heat. Add more water if necessary to cover all the ingredients completely. Bring to a boil. Reduce heat and simmer, uncovered, for 1½ hours, or until the water is reduced by half. Skim off any surface sediment or fat.

2.   Strain the stock into a container using a strainer to remove the chicken and vegetables. Refrigerate for up to 3 days or store in an airtight, freezer-safe container for up to 1 month.

Keep Rotisserie Domes

Most store-bought rotisserie chicken comes in a plastic dome that can be used as a mini greenhouse to start seeds. Before you recycle them, reuse them to start fresh herbs or lettuce for your culinary use.

Vegetable Stock

Vegetable stock is great to use in place of water to add extra flavor to rice and mashed potatoes. This recipe doesn't include salt, so add salt to the final meal at your discretion. You probably only need a pinch.

4 CUPS

2 teaspoons extra-virgin olive oil

1 small yellow onion, chopped

4 cloves garlic, minced

1 stalk celery, with leafy top, chopped

1 large carrot, peeled and chopped

3 green onions, sliced

1 bay leaf

4 sprigs fresh flat-leaf parsley

2 sprigs fresh thyme

4 cups cold water

1. Heat the oil in a large stockpot on medium-high. Add the vegetables and herbs. Cook for 5 minutes, stirring frequently.

2. Add the water and bring to a boil. Reduce heat to low and simmer, uncovered, for 45 minutes.

3. Remove from heat and allow to cool, about 1 hour. Strain and discard the vegetables. Store the stock in a large jar in the refrigerator until ready to use or store in a freezer-safe container for up to 1 month.

Make the Most of Your Purchase

If you find that you have leftover ingredients from a recipe, use the remaining ingredients to make another recipe before the ingredients go bad. When you're a busy parent, the days go by so fast and it's easy to forget to use up the celery (or even that you bought celery to begin with) or mango from the last grocery trip. It requires a little planning, but your hard-earned money and valuable time won't go to waste.

Too Good Tomato Soup

If you have a 15-ounce can of organic diced tomatoes in the pantry, you can certainly use that in place of the fresh tomatoes in this recipe. For a nutritional boost, try adding whole-wheat pasta shapes such as stars or alphabets.

6 SERVINGS

2 large tomatoes, chopped

½ cup vegetable stock (store-bought or homemade—see the recipe in this chapter)

¼ teaspoon dried oregano

¼ teaspoon dried basil

¼ teaspoon salt

⅛ teaspoon ground black pepper

2 cups whole milk

2 tablespoons tomato paste

1. Heat the tomatoes, stock, oregano, basil, salt, and pepper in a medium saucepan over medium heat. Cover.

2. Gently bring to a boil and cook for 10 minutes. Remove from heat. Let cool for about 5 minutes.

3. Purée the mixture in a blender for about 30 seconds. Set aside.

4. Add the milk and tomato paste to the saucepan. Stir to combine.

5. Add the purée to the saucepan. Cook over medium heat, stirring occasionally for about 5 minutes. Serve warm.

Vitamin-Packed Tomatoes

Tomatoes provide vitamin C, potassium, fiber, and lycopene, which helps keep the heart and eyes healthy. The riper the tomato, the higher the levels of lycopene it contains.

Super Egg Salad

Egg salad can be served a variety of ways. Add a serving of whole grains by making a sandwich with whole-wheat bread, or serve it inside pita bread, on crackers, or by itself. No matter what you decide, your child will benefit from the nutritional value of eggs and will get a nice serving of vegetables too.

4 SERVINGS

2 hard-boiled eggs, chopped

¾ cup steamed and chopped cauliflower

¼ cup peeled and grated carrot

¼ cup chopped yellow onion

¼ cup chopped celery

2 teaspoons prepared yellow mustard

3 tablespoons mayonnaise

⅛ teaspoon salt

⅛ teaspoon ground black pepper

Mix together all the ingredients in a medium bowl. Chill in the refrigerator for 15 minutes. Serve. Refrigerate leftovers for up to 3 days.

What Makes Eggs So Healthy?

Eggs are healthy for your body. One egg provides 6 grams of protein and provides vitamin A, B vitamins, potassium, folic acid, and biotin. They're also good for your budget—compared to other animal-based proteins, they're much less expensive.

Crunchy Green Beans

This recipe is similar to traditional green bean casserole, but the preparation is a lot faster and the texture is crunchier.

6 SERVINGS
··············

3 cups fresh string beans, trimmed

3 tablespoons extra-virgin olive oil, divided

1 cup corn flakes, crushed

Kosher salt and ground black pepper, to taste

1. Steam the beans in a double boiler until tender, about 10 minutes.

2. Meanwhile, add 1 tablespoon of the olive oil to a large skillet and brown the crushed corn flakes over medium-low heat. Transfer the corn flakes to a small bowl and set aside.

3. Add the steamed green beans, salt, pepper, and remaining olive oil to the same skillet. Sauté over medium-high heat for about 3–4 minutes, until heated through.

4. Transfer the beans to a bowl with a slotted spoon.

5. Top the green beans with the corn flakes (or mix together if desired) and serve.

Grilled Cheese Squares

This is a traditional favorite among many children. Serve it with Too Good Tomato Soup and Chunky Cherry Applesauce (see the recipes in this chapter) for a balanced meal.

4 SERVINGS
....

2 tablespoons unsalted butter, divided

2 slices whole-wheat bread

2 slices mild Cheddar cheese

1. Generously butter one side of both slices of bread. Cut off the crusts with a knife.

2. Preheat a skillet over medium heat. Place a slice of bread butter-side-down on the skillet. Top with the cheese. Place the other slice of bread butter-side-up on top of the cheese. Cook for 1–2 minutes, or until golden brown on the bottom. Use a spatula to flip the sandwich, and cook the other side for 1–2 minutes, or until golden brown.

3. Remove from heat and let stand for about 2 minutes. Cut the sandwich into 4 squares. Let cool slightly before serving. Serve warm.

My First Fruit Salad with Yogurt Sauce

For best results, use super ripe cantaloupe. It's softer, so easier for young children to chew. This fruit combination is great for beginners.

8 SERVINGS

1 cup diced cantaloupe (1" dice)

1 cup diced watermelon (1" dice)

1 cup diced strawberries

1 cup sliced and quartered bananas

¾ cup full-fat vanilla yogurt

¼ cup heavy cream

2 tablespoons granulated
sugar, or to taste

½ teaspoon pure vanilla extract

1. Combine all the fruit in a bowl.

2. Whisk together the yogurt, heavy cream, sugar, and vanilla extract in a small bowl. Pour into a serving dish. Serve the fruit chunks with the dipping sauce on the side.

Peach Applesauce

Chances are, you won't find organic peach applesauce at the store. This is a recipe that my kids and I created with ingredients we had on hand one day. Ahh . . . one of the joys of making healthy organic meals from scratch!

12 SERVINGS

5 Fuji or Gala apples, peeled, cored, and chopped

1 cup skinned and chopped peaches

¼ cup apple or white grape juice

1 teaspoon pure vanilla extract

¼ teaspoon ground cinnamon (optional)

2 tablespoons turbinado sugar (optional)

1. Combine all the ingredients in a large pot. Bring to a boil.

2. Cook on medium-high heat for about 10–15 minutes, until the fruit is tender, stirring occasionally.

3. Mash with a potato masher until a coarse texture is reached. For a smooth consistency, purée the mixture in a blender for 30–60 seconds.

4. Serve warm or chilled. Refrigerate leftovers for up to 5 days or freeze for up to 1 month.

Seriously? Canned Peaches Are More Nutritious?

A study conducted by Oregon State University shows that canned cling peaches have a lot more vitamin C, vitamin A, folate, and antioxidants than fresh peaches due to the canning process. So don't snub your nose at organic canned cling peaches!

Chunky Cherry Applesauce

If you don't have fresh cherries on hand, you can also substitute frozen cherries or even cherry preserves. If you use cherry preserves, reduce the amount to ½ cup.

6 SERVINGS

5 Fuji or Gala apples, peeled, cored, and chopped

¾ cup pitted and chopped Bing or Rainier cherries

¼ cup apple or white grape juice

2 tablespoons turbinado sugar (optional)

1. Combine all the ingredients in a medium saucepan. Bring to a boil.

2. Cook on medium-high heat for about 10–15 minutes, or until tender, stirring occasionally.

3. Mash with a potato masher until a coarse texture is reached. For a smooth consistency, purée the mixture in a blender for 30–60 seconds.

4. Serve warm or chilled. Refrigerate leftovers for up to 5 days.

Cherries Are All the Rage

Cherries are loaded with potassium and protective antioxidants that fight against cancer. The darker and riper the cherry, the more antioxidants it contains. Load up on these ruby jewels.

Kale Toscana

Kale has become very popular these days, giving collard greens a run for their money. While both provide an abundance of vitamins, minerals, and antioxidants, kale is higher in vitamin K, which your growing toddler needs for good bone health.

6 SERVINGS

2 slices pork bacon, diced

½ pound pork breakfast sausage

½ small yellow onion, finely chopped

1 clove garlic, minced

1½ cups chopped fresh kale (stems removed)

2 cups chicken stock (store-bought or homemade—see the recipe in this chapter)

1 large russet potato, peeled and thinly sliced

½ teaspoon salt

¼ teaspoon ground black pepper

¾ cup whole milk

1. Heat a large pot or Dutch oven over medium-high heat. Add the bacon and cook until crisp. Drain the fat from the bacon into a small bowl using a fine-mesh strainer. Reserve 1 tablespoon of the bacon drippings and discard the rest. Transfer the bacon to a small bowl.

2. Crumble the sausage with your hands and cook in the same pot over medium-high heat until browned. Drain off the fat and transfer the sausage to a small bowl.

3. Add the reserved bacon fat to the pot. (You can also use 1 tablespoon olive oil if you prefer.) Add the onion and garlic and sauté over medium heat until tender. Stir in the kale and cook until it begins to wilt.

4. Add the chicken stock, potato, bacon, sausage, salt, and pepper. Stir to combine. Increase heat to medium-high and bring to a boil. Cover. Cook for 10 minutes, stirring occasionally.

5. Reduce heat to low and add the milk. Simmer for 10 minutes, stirring occasionally. Serve immediately.

Orzo Harmony

It is common to mistake orzo for rice because they look like twins, but orzo is actually a pasta. It's a great choice for babies mastering the art of chewing. This dish is certainly one that guarantees your self-feeder will grab a handful.

4 SERVINGS

2 cups water or vegetable stock
(store-bought or homemade—
see the recipe in this chapter)

¾ cup orzo pasta

1 tablespoon unsalted butter

3 tablespoons chopped
fresh flat-leaf parsley

3 tablespoons chopped fresh chives

3 tablespoons lemon juice

½ cup chopped broccoli florets

1. In a small saucepan, bring the water or stock to a boil.

2. Add the orzo and cook for about 5–7 minutes, or until al dente. Drain all but a few tablespoons of liquid to prevent the pasta from sticking together.

3. In a medium mixing bowl, toss together the butter, parsley, chives, lemon juice, broccoli, and orzo to coat.

4. Serve warm or cold. Refrigerate leftovers for up to 3 days.

Stock-Full of Flavor!
Consider substituting chicken or vegetable stock for plain water in savory recipes. Not only do you boost nutritional content, but you also boost the flavor factor. This technique is particularly useful for anything that is boiled, like rice, pasta, or potatoes.

Rigatoni Marinara

The beef in this recipe provides iron for healthy growth and development. Children need iron at this age, since their iron stores start to deplete at around 6 months old.

4 SERVINGS

1 cup rigatoni pasta

1 tablespoon extra-virgin olive oil

1 clove garlic, minced

¼ cup diced green bell pepper

4 ounces lean ground beef

¼ teaspoon salt

⅛ teaspoon ground black pepper

1½ cups marinara sauce (store-bought or homemade—see the recipe in this chapter)

1 tablespoon chopped fresh flat-leaf parsley

1. Cook the pasta according to package directions. Keep warm.

2. Meanwhile, in a large pan, heat the olive oil on medium-high. Add the garlic, bell pepper, ground beef, salt, and pepper. Cook until the beef is no longer pink, breaking it into small pieces with a spoon. Drain excess fat.

3. Combine the marinara sauce with the meat mixture. Add the parsley. Cook until heated through, about 5 minutes.

4. To serve, spoon sauce over a small serving of pasta in a bowl. Mix to combine. Refrigerate leftovers promptly for up to 3 days or freeze for up to 2 weeks.

Pimento Mac and Cheese

Pimentos are small, red, sweet chili peppers, also known as cherry peppers. Their sweet flavor adds a nice touch to traditional mac and cheese and their bright red color adds interest that little ones enjoy.

8 SERVINGS

4 cups water

2 cups elbow macaroni

3 tablespoons unsalted butter

2½ tablespoons unbleached all-purpose flour

1 teaspoon dry mustard

½ teaspoon salt

¼ teaspoon ground black pepper

3 cups whole milk

2 cups shredded sharp Cheddar cheese

2 cups shredded mild Cheddar cheese

1 (4-ounce) jar chopped pimentos, drained

1. In a medium saucepan, bring the water to a boil. Add the macaroni. Cook until al dente, about 7 minutes. Drain in a strainer. Set aside.

2. Melt the butter in a medium pot over medium heat; whisk in the flour, mustard, salt, and pepper. Cook for 1 minute, whisking constantly.

3. Gradually whisk in the milk, then the cheese. Whisk constantly until the cheese is no longer stringy, about 2 minutes. Add the pasta and pimentos. Stir to coat. Cover. Note: The mixture will be soupy at first but will thicken.

4. Reduce heat and simmer on low for 20 minutes or until thickened, stirring occasionally. Remove from heat. Serve warm.

Enriched vs. Whole-Wheat Pasta

Enriched pasta—the basic pasta in stores—consists of refined grains that are enriched by adding nutrients back into the pasta by the manufacturer. Whole-wheat pasta is made with the whole kernel of the grain which provides fiber, B vitamins, and a rich amount of trace minerals. Research shows that a diet rich in whole grains can prevent illness and disease and maintain a healthy body.

Marinara Sauce

This simple sauce can be used to accompany many meals and snacks, like Mozzarella Sticks, Parmesan Chicken Skillet, or Italian Herbed Spaghetti Squash (see the recipes in Chapter 5).

8 SERVINGS

¼ cup extra-virgin olive oil

2 large cloves garlic, minced

1 small yellow onion, finely chopped

¼ cup chopped fresh flat-leaf parsley

1 teaspoon kosher salt

¼ teaspoon ground black pepper

1 teaspoon dried oregano

1 teaspoon dried basil

2 (14.5-ounce) cans crushed tomatoes, drained

1 (6-ounce) can tomato paste

½ cup chicken stock (store-bought or homemade—see the recipe in this chapter)

1 tablespoon light brown sugar

1. In a large pot, heat the oil on medium. Sauté the garlic and onion until the onion is translucent and fragrant, about 8–10 minutes.

2. Add the remaining ingredients and mix well.

3. Simmer on low heat for 1 hour, stirring occasionally. Serve as a dip or pasta sauce. Refrigerate for up to 5 days or freeze for up to 1 month.

> ### BPA in Canned Tomatoes
> Bisphenol A (BPA) is an industrial chemical used in the linings of metal cans to prevent corrosion. BPA may cause adverse health effects in infants and children. If you're concerned about BPA in canned tomatoes or other produce, look for brands that use BPA-free liners (specified on the can) or choose canned products in glass jars to avoid the issue altogether. If you are unsure if your favorite brand contains BPA, e-mail the company directly to find out.

Timeless Minestrone Soup

Minestrone soup is a one-pot wonder filled with all types of goodness. It's best to introduce it to toddlers soon after transitioning from purées, while the flavor profile of vegetables is still on the tip of their tongue.

8 SERVINGS

5 cups water

1 zucchini, cubed

1 carrot, peeled and chopped

½ (15-ounce) can white beans, drained

½ cup elbow macaroni

½ (28-ounce) can plum tomatoes

1 teaspoon dried parsley

1 teaspoon dried oregano

½ teaspoon salt, or to taste

¼ teaspoon ground black pepper, or to taste

⅓ cup grated Parmesan cheese

1. In a large saucepan over medium-high heat, bring the water to a boil.

2. Add the zucchini, carrot, white beans, and macaroni. Return to a boil.

3. Add the tomatoes with their juice. Return to a boil.

4. Stir in the parsley, oregano, salt, and pepper.

5. Reduce heat to medium-low, cover, and simmer for 10 minutes or until the zucchini is tender and the macaroni is cooked. Pour the soup into serving bowls and garnish with the Parmesan cheese. Refrigerate for up to 3 days.

Straining Soup for the Little Guys

If your little one can't use a spoon yet, or you're not able to spoon-feed him, drain out the liquid from his portion using a strainer and serve him the rest of the soup on his highchair tray. He gets all the "parts" of the soup but he can eat it with his hands. It's also a good way to serve one dish to the whole family—those who can use spoons can eat it that way, but your toddler can just use his hands.

South of the Border Taco Bowl

Here's a great timesaving tip: Cook ground beef ahead of time and freeze in 4-ounce portions so that when you want to make something quick, the ground beef is already done and other ingredients can be added to make a quick meal. Add Traditional Salsa (Chapter 6) to this recipe for a flavor boost and an extra dose of lycopene.

2 SERVINGS

2 tablespoons extra-virgin olive oil

1 tablespoon diced yellow onion

**1 tablespoon diced
green bell pepper**

4 ounces lean ground beef

1 tablespoon tomato paste

1 tablespoon water

⅛ teaspoon ground cumin

Pinch of kosher salt

½ cup cooked brown rice

2 tablespoons shredded
Cheddar cheese

2 tablespoons crushed tortilla chips

1. Drizzle the olive oil in a medium skillet over medium heat. Add the onion and bell pepper and sauté until tender.

2. Add the ground beef and cook until browned. Drain excess fat.

3. Stir in the tomato paste, water, cumin, and salt, and rice. Mix well. Reduce heat to low and simmer for 10 minutes.

4. Sprinkle the shredded cheese over the meat mixture. Stir until just melted. To serve, scoop a portion into a bowl and top with crushed tortilla chips.

What's in Your Bell Pepper?

Bell peppers come in a variety of colors including red, yellow, orange, and green. Each offers a slightly different nutritional profile of antioxidants and different degrees of flavor depending on the ripeness. Green bell peppers are more tart and yellow, red, and orange bell peppers are usually sweeter. For maximum nutrition, use a variety of peppers in recipes.

Chicken Corn Chowder

When you've got a ton of chicken in the freezer that you need to do something with, make a chowder. Have you ever heard of a freezer party? It's when you cook up everything in the freezer before it gets that dreadful freezer burn. Remember all the chicken stock you made and froze? Oh, and the leftover chicken breast that's forming ice crystals as we speak? Throw it all in a pot to make this chowder for your toddler.

8 SERVINGS
. . . .
2 teaspoons extra-virgin olive oil

1 small yellow onion, diced

¼ cup diced red bell pepper

¼ cup diced celery

1½ cups chicken stock (store-bought or homemade—see the recipe in this chapter)

1 cup whole milk

1 cup shredded cooked chicken breast

1½ cups frozen corn kernels

⅛ teaspoon dried thyme

¼ teaspoon salt

⅛ teaspoon ground black pepper

¼ cup chopped fresh flat-leaf parsley

1. Heat the olive oil in a saucepan over medium heat. Add the onion, red pepper, and celery. Sauté until tender, about 2 minutes.

2. Add the chicken stock, milk, shredded chicken, corn, thyme, salt, and pepper. Simmer for 15 minutes.

3. Stir in the fresh parsley. Serve hot.

Cool Pasta Salad

Pasta is a wonderful finger food for toddlers. This Cool Pasta Salad can be eaten with tiny fingers, but keep a bib handy—things can get a little messy! This pasta offers whole grains and a boatload of colorful veggies. You can also chop up a hard-boiled egg to add more protein to this meal.

8 SERVINGS

1 cup whole-wheat rotini
or mini farfalle pasta

1 tablespoon extra-virgin olive oil

¼ cup mayonnaise

¼ cup sour cream

2 teaspoons dried Italian seasoning

½ teaspoon garlic powder

¼ cup diced green bell pepper

¼ cup chopped broccoli florets

¼ cup diced red bell pepper

¼ cup peeled and grated carrot

¼ cup diced Vidalia onion

Salt and ground black pepper to taste

1. Cook the pasta according to package directions. Rinse with cold water to stop the pasta from cooking. Drain and place in the refrigerator to cool.

2. Meanwhile, prepare the dressing by whisking together the olive oil, mayonnaise, sour cream, Italian seasoning, and garlic powder in small bowl. Set aside.

3. Combine the pasta and prepared dressing. Add the vegetables and salt and pepper to taste. Serve chilled. Refrigerate for up to 3 days.

Woodland Mushroom Risotto

Risotto is similar to rice, but it has a chewier texture. Transitioners can get some chewing practice with this dish, but they don't need a full set of teeth for risotto—just a few will do the job.

6 SERVINGS
. . . .

3 tablespoons extra-virgin olive oil

1½ cups sliced assorted fresh mushrooms

½ teaspoon dried thyme

1 cup Arborio rice

4 cups vegetable stock (store-bought or homemade—see the recipe in this chapter)

1 cup grated Parmesan cheese

2 tablespoons unsalted butter

1. Heat the olive oil in a large saucepan over medium heat. When hot, add the mushrooms and thyme. Cook and stir until the mushrooms give up their liquid and it evaporates, about 6–8 minutes. Stir in the rice; cook and stir for 3–4 minutes, until the rice is opaque.

2. Meanwhile, heat the vegetable stock in another saucepan over low heat.

3. Add the heated stock to the rice mixture about 1 cup at a time, stirring until absorbed.

4. After all the stock is added and the rice is tender, remove from heat. Stir in the cheese and butter, cover, and let stand for 5 minutes. Stir, then serve immediately.

Lots of Mushroom Varieties and Benefits Too

Mushrooms provide important nutrients such as potassium, riboflavin, niacin, vitamin D, manganese, copper, zinc, and more. Portobello, cremini, button, chanterelle, shiitake, and porcini mushrooms are available at most grocery or health food stores. Pick a combination of mushrooms for a rich, deep, earthy flavor in just about any recipe. To clean them, simply brush them with a towel, then chop and throw 'em in the pot.

Chilled White Grape Peach Soup

Chilled soups are a favorite in my home, especially in hot months. For best results, freeze the grapes whole for at least 8 hours. Serve this soup with a couple of whole-grain or gluten-free crackers and Cheddar cheese cubes.

4 SERVINGS

1 cup white seedless grapes, frozen

½ cup sliced frozen peaches

¼ cup full-fat vanilla yogurt

¼ cup white grape juice

1. Combine all the ingredients in a blender and blend until smooth, about 45 seconds.

2. Transfer the soup to a small bowl. Serve chilled.

Simply Quinoa

Quinoa doesn't really have much of a flavor by itself, but it takes on the flavor of whatever it's prepared with. Not only is quinoa easy to prepare and store, but it is also a great source of protein and healthy fat.

6–8 SERVINGS

½ cup uncooked quinoa, rinsed

1½ cups chicken stock or vegetable stock (store-bought or homemade—see the recipes in this chapter)

1½ tablespoons coconut oil

⅛ teaspoon salt, or to taste

⅛ teaspoon ground black pepper

1. Add the quinoa and stock (or water) to a saucepan over high heat. Bring to a boil.

2. Reduce heat to low, cover, and cook for about 15 minutes, or until all the liquid is absorbed.

3. Stir in the coconut oil, salt, and pepper. Serve hot or cold.

Slow Cooker Baby Lima Beans

Beans are wonderful for babies because they are an excellent source of iron, fiber, protein, and manganese for metabolism and bone development. The smoked meat adds a boost of flavor to make the baby lima beans tasty.

4 SERVINGS

1 cup dried baby lima beans

½ cup chopped smoked turkey meat

3 cups chicken stock, as needed
(store-bought or homemade—
see the recipe in this chapter)

¼ cup chopped yellow onion

¼ teaspoon of seasoned pepper
or ground black pepper

1. Wash the beans in a colander. Inspect the beans to ensure there are no little rocks or bad beans in the batch.

2. Add the turkey meat to a slow cooker with enough chicken stock to cover the meat. Bring to a slow simmer over medium heat.

3. Add the beans, onion, and pepper. Add more stock to cover as needed. Increase the heat to high, cover, and cook for 6 hours. Serve.

Where to Buy Smoked Turkey
You can find smoked turkey breast or leg in the poultry section of many grocery stores that carry organic meat. You can also find smoked turkey at local farmers' markets where meat is sold.

Sautéed Kale

Sautéed kale is great alone as a side dish or mixed with any type of whole-wheat pasta or rice. Add cubed chicken or turkey for a complete meal.

2 SERVINGS
• • • • • • • • • • • • • •

2 tablespoons extra-virgin olive oil

**2 cups chopped kale
(stems removed)**

½ teaspoon Kosher salt, or to taste

¼ teaspoon ground black pepper

¼ teaspoon onion powder

¼ teaspoon garlic powder

Heat the oil in a large sauté pan. Add all the ingredients. Sauté the kale until tender, about 5–7 minutes. Serve immediately.

All-American Burger Dogs

Toddlers love hot dogs! Instead of serving a processed hot dog, offer loose ground beef or chicken while still using a hot dog bun, which kids love. It looks like a hot dog, but it is much better for them (and isn't a choking hazard, either).

8 SERVINGS
....

1 pound lean ground beef
or ground chicken

½ teaspoon kosher salt

¼ teaspoon ground black pepper

½ small yellow onion, chopped

2 tablespoons prepared yellow mustard

2 tablespoons ketchup

1 heaping tablespoon sweet relish

½ cup shredded Cheddar cheese

8 whole-wheat hot dog buns

1. Add the ground beef or chicken to a skillet over medium-high heat. Add the salt, pepper, onion, mustard, ketchup, and relish. Mix well. Cook until the meat is no longer pink, about 8–10 minutes. Drain off the fat using a fine-mesh strainer.

2. Return the mixture to the pan and stir in the shredded cheese. Cook for about 2 minutes, until heated through.

3. Scoop a couple tablespoons of the meat mixture into each hot dog bun. Cut each bun into thirds. Serve immediately.

Stuffed Cabbage with Gravy

Traditionally, stuffed cabbage is served with a tomato-based sauce, but this version is prepared by making a roux for gravy. Feel free to use ground beef, chicken, or turkey instead of lamb.

16 SERVINGS

1 medium head green cabbage

1 pound ground lamb

1 cup cooked brown rice

¼ teaspoon garlic powder

Pinch of ground black pepper

Pinch of ground coriander (optional)

2 large eggs

GRAVY

3 tablespoons unsalted butter

2 tablespoons unbleached all-purpose flour

2 cups chicken stock (store-bought or homemade—see the recipe in this chapter)

1. Preheat oven to 350°F.

2. Remove the core from the cabbage with a knife. Remove the outer leaves. Add to a large pot.

3. Add enough water to cover the leaves. Bring to a boil. Cook for about 1–2 minutes, until just softened. Place the leaves in a bowl of ice water to stop the cooking process. Set aside.

4. In a separate bowl, combine the lamb, rice, garlic powder, pepper, coriander, and eggs. Mix well.

5. Place a small amount of the mixture into the center of each leaf and fold the sides of the leaf inward to resemble a roll. Place each roll in a 9" × 13" baking dish.

6. To make the gravy, melt the butter in a medium skillet over medium-high heat. Add the flour and stir until dark brown. Add the chicken stock. Stir until thickened.

7. Pour the gravy over the cabbage rolls. Bake for 45 minutes. Serve.

Skillet Apples

These skillet apples are quick to prepare and have a subtle coconut flavor, which adds a nice twist to tra-ditional skillet apples. Serve alongside chicken or pork or add a dollop of frozen yogurt for a sweet treat.

8 SERVINGS
. . . .

2 tablespoons coconut oil or unsalted butter

4 Fuji or Gala apples, peeled, cored, and chopped

¼ cup light brown sugar

⅛ teaspoon ground cinnamon

⅛ teaspoon ground nutmeg

1. Melt the coconut oil or butter in a large skillet over medium heat. Add the apples, brown sugar, cinnamon, and nutmeg.

2. Stirring occasionally, cook until tender, about 10 min-utes. Serve warm. Refrigerate leftovers or freeze for up to 2 weeks.

Fruit Parfait

You can use any type of organic cereal for this parfait. It offers a bit of crunch alongside the smooth yogurt, which is an interesting texture combination for new eaters.

2 SERVINGS
. . . .

½ cup full-fat strawberry yogurt

¼ cup diced strawberries

¼ cup diced banana

¼ cup cereal O's

Fill the bottoms of 2 small serving cups or bowls with 1 tablespoon yogurt each. Alternate layers of bananas, strawberries, and cereal with yogurt until almost filled, reserving some yogurt and cereal for the top. Serve.

CHAPTER 5
THE EXPLORER —
12 TO 18 MONTHS

Explorers need plenty of freedom to touch, smell, and taste food with their hands, and they need lots of eating practice using a spoon. Engage them during shopping trips with plenty of opportunities to pick up fruit and vegetables and talk about the wonderful meals you are planning. While you are cooking, give your child a few safe kitchen items to play with, such as a whisk, mixing bowl, and play food so that she can have her own cooking experience!

Adventures await for toddler explorers at every turn. Your child is very active during this age and needs about 1,000 calories per day, so it's important to provide energy-rich snacks consisting of whole grains, fruit, and vegetables, between meals. This chapter includes lots of energizing snack recipes to get your child through the day. "Grazing" is still normal at this age, so if your child doesn't eat everything you offer, save it for later when he's hungry. Don't offer any treats until he's had a nutritious meal to prevent him from loading up on empty calories.

IMPORTANT TIPS TO REMEMBER FOR THE EXPLORER

- Cow's milk can now be introduced as the primary milk source unless your child has dietary restrictions. However, limit the intake to 16–20 ounces since most of her calories will come from solids.
- If your child cannot drink cow's milk, discuss the best nondairy option with his pediatrician.
- Ditch the bottles and use sippy cups to teach drinking from a real cup.
- Offer water to quench thirst. If you offer juice, dilute it with 50 percent water and limit intake to 4 ounces per day.
- Reduce choking risks by cutting everything you offer into small, easily chewable pieces.

Dutch Baked Apple Pancake

Pancakes and apple filling are a match made in heaven. Skip the syrup—the apple filling is more than sweet enough.

8 SERVINGS

APPLE FILLING

2 tablespoons unsalted butter

3–4 Fuji or Gala apples, peeled, cored, and thinly sliced

6 tablespoons granulated sugar

1 teaspoon ground cinnamon

PANCAKE BATTER

3 large eggs

½ cup unbleached all-purpose flour

½ cup 2% milk

1 tablespoon full-fat plain yogurt

1 teaspoon grated lemon zest

1. Preheat oven to 400°F. In a large skillet, melt the butter.

2. Add the sliced apples, sugar, and cinnamon. Sauté and continue stirring until the apples are soft. Remove from heat. Transfer the apples to a large, round pie pan and set aside.

3. Beat the eggs until foamy. Add the flour, milk, yogurt, and lemon zest and beat until smooth. Pour the pancake batter over the apples.

4. Bake for 25 minutes, until puffy and golden brown.

Fried Egg Sizzler

Fried eggs were famous in my family as a child. The crispy egg white is so delicious. Toddlers may or may not enjoy the slippery yolk, but it's worth a try! Remember, cooking foods different ways may yield different results—so if he doesn't like scrambled eggs, try this fried egg. Serve with whole-wheat toast, a sippy cup of milk, and fresh fruit.

1 SERVING

1 large egg

2–3 teaspoons canola oil

Salt and ground black pepper, to taste

1. Crack egg into a small bowl, being careful not to break the yolk.

2. Heat the canola oil in a small nonstick pan over medium heat until just hot. Swirl the oil around the pan to coat evenly. Oil will become a shimmery gloss when it's hot.

3. Carefully pour the egg into the hot oil. Let the egg sizzle for about 1 minute undisturbed. Spoon the hot oil from the pan onto the egg white. Reduce heat to low. Sprinkle with salt and pepper. Cook until the yolk is firm. Serve immediately.

Make Eggs Over Easy

To make eggs over easy, follow all the steps in the fried egg recipe. However, at the end, carefully flip the entire egg over with a spatula and cook the other side for 1–2 minutes longer.

Butterscotch Oatmeal

The brown sugar and milk gives this oatmeal a butterscotch flavor. It's certainly one of those "stick to your ribs" type of meals that I like to give my children to keep them full all morning.

4 SERVINGS
....

2 cups whole milk

1 large egg, beaten

2 tablespoons light brown sugar

¼ teaspoon ground cinnamon

1 cup quick-cooking oats

2 teaspoons unsalted butter (optional)

1. Add the milk, egg, and brown sugar to a pot over medium-low heat. Gradually turn up the heat to medium-high, stirring constantly. (Be careful not to turn up the heat to high, or you'll scrambled the egg.)

2. Stir in the oats and add the butter, if desired. Heat until bubbly. Serve immediately.

Top It Off

Try incorporating a little ground flaxseed into breakfast cereals, including granola, and baked goods. Flaxseed is a great source of omega-3s, fiber, and antioxidants. For example, sprinkle 1 teaspoon on this oatmeal.

Two-Berry Parfait

Strawberries and raspberries unite in this red and white parfait filled with calcium and antioxidants.

2 SERVINGS

½ cup full-fat strawberry yogurt

½ cup whipped cream (store-bought or homemade—see the recipe in this chapter)

½ cup chopped strawberries

¼ cup chopped raspberries

1. Combine the yogurt and whipped cream in a small bowl. Set aside.

2. In 2 small serving cups, layer the ingredients in this order: strawberries, yogurt, raspberries, yogurt. Repeat, then top with a mixture of both strawberries and raspberries, and whipped cream, if desired.

Organic Raspberries Reign Supreme
According to the Worlds Healthiest Foods (*www.whfoods.org*), organic raspberries are significantly higher in antioxidants than nonorganic raspberries. Purchase fully ripened raspberries for maximum antioxidant benefits, keep them refrigerated, and consume them within 1–2 days after purchase.

Scrumptious Prune Muffins

Incorporating prunes into muffins is a great way to introduce prunes to toddlers. Prunes have lots of fiber, which can keep their digestive systems moving.

12 SERVINGS

1 large egg

½ cup turbinado sugar

¼ cup canola oil

1½ teaspoons pure vanilla extract

1 cup mashed banana

1½ cups unbleached all-purpose flour

1 teaspoon baking soda

1 teaspoon baking powder

¼ teaspoon ground cinnamon

1 cup chopped prunes

1. Preheat oven to 350°F. Generously grease and flour a standard 12-cup muffin pan.

2. In a large bowl, whisk the egg, sugar, oil, and vanilla until smooth. Fold in the banana.

3. In a separate bowl, combine the flour, baking soda, baking powder, and cinnamon. Mix in the prunes.

4. Stir the dry ingredients into the egg mixture and mix until just moistened. Spoon into the muffin cups.

5. Bake for 20–25 minutes, or until a toothpick inserted into the center of a muffin comes out clean. Freeze for up to 2 weeks.

Are Turbinado and Brown Sugar the Same Thing?

Turbinado sugar is a partially processed brown sugar that maintains a light gold-ish color and larger crystals. Light and dark brown sugar have a stronger molasses taste than turbinado because they retain more of the molasses syrup that is produced during processing. Therefore if you substitute turbinado for light or dark brown sugar (or dark for light, for that matter) in a recipe you may get a slightly different flavor or different results altogether.

Fiesta Omelet

This omelet is a step up for Transitioners used to scrambled eggs. Serve with whole-wheat toast and a sippy cup of whole milk.

2 SERVINGS
....

2 large eggs, beaten

1 tablespoon whole milk

Pinch of salt and ground black pepper

1 tablespoon unsalted butter

3 tablespoons salsa (store-bought or homemade—see the recipe in Chapter 6)

¼ cup shredded Cheddar cheese

1. Beat the eggs with the milk, salt, and pepper. Set aside.

2. Melt the butter in a medium skillet over medium heat. Swirl the skillet to coat with butter. When the butter starts to bubble, add the egg mixture and cook for about 4–5 minutes or until the egg begins to set in the center and around the edges.

3. Spoon the salsa in the center and sprinkle with cheese. Use a spatula to gently fold one edge of the omelet over to the other side. Cook until the cheese melts.

4. Slide the omelet onto a plate. Cut into bite-size pieces and serve.

Hummus

Authentic hummus is made with tahini, a paste made of ground sesame seeds. It adds a rich flavor and smooth, creamy texture to any recipe. You can make hummus without it, but then it wouldn't be the real deal!

8 SERVINGS

4 cloves garlic

2 tablespoons extra-virgin olive oil, plus more for serving

¼ cup tahini

1 large lemon, juiced

½ teaspoon Kosher salt

1 (15-ounce) can chickpeas (garbanzo beans), drained

Pinch of paprika, for serving

1. Peel the garlic cloves but leave them whole. Place the garlic in a small, heavy skillet along with the olive oil. Cook over medium heat until the garlic turns light brown, stirring frequently, for about 5–8 minutes; watch carefully to ensure it doesn't burn. Remove from heat and let cool for 10 minutes.

2. Combine the garlic and oil with the remaining ingredients (except the paprika) in a food processor and process until smooth.

3. Spread on a serving plate, drizzle with a bit more olive oil, and sprinkle with paprika. Serve with vegetables or pita chips. Refrigerate leftovers for up to 4 days.

Chilled Strawberry Refresher

Depending on how sweet your strawberries are, you may or may not need to add honey to this recipe. If you purchase frozen strawberries in the bag, there is no way to tell beforehand. However, if you pick and freeze your own, you can generally get a sense of how sweet the crop is by tasting one before you freeze them. In either case, use your best judgment for adding the honey—you don't want this refresher to be overly sweet.

2 SERVINGS

½ cup frozen strawberries

¼ cup full-fat vanilla yogurt

2 tablespoons honey (optional)

¼ cup apple juice

1. Combine all the ingredients in a blender and blend until smooth.

2. Serve chilled in a small cup with a straw.

Use Eco-friendly Reusable Straws

Instead of purchasing disposable plastic straws that you can only use once, look for reusable stainless-steel straws that can be washed and reused over and over. You'll save a little money and the environment will benefit too.

Cheese Pizza-Dillas

Feel free to jazz up these basic pizza-dillas using shredded chicken, ground beef, onions, mushrooms, peppers, or anything you have on hand. Serve with a salad and fresh fruit.

4 SERVINGS
. . . .

2 (8") whole-wheat flour tortillas

1 tablespoon unsalted butter

½ cup pizza sauce (store-bought or homemade—see the recipe in Chapter 7)

¾ cup shredded mozzarella cheese, or more if desired

1. Generously butter one side of each tortilla.

2. Heat a flat skillet over medium heat. Place a tortilla butter-side down on the skillet. Quickly spoon the pizza sauce on top, about 1" from the edge. Sprinkle the cheese on top.

3. Place the other tortilla butter-side up on top of the cheese. Once the bottom is lightly golden, flip the tortilla using a large spatula. Cook until lightly golden. Cut into quarters with a pizza cutter. Serve.

Savory Herbed Chicken Breasts

There is actually enough chicken in this recipe to serve a family of four, including the baby. However, if you want to plan ahead, freeze the remaining breasts to save time in the future. Each chicken breast makes 4 toddler servings.

16 SERVINGS

1 tablespoon extra-virgin olive oil

1 tablespoon unsalted butter

1 clove garlic, cut in half

2 tablespoons lemon juice

2 tablespoons chopped
fresh flat-leaf parsley

¼ teaspoon dried thyme

¼ teaspoon salt

⅛ teaspoon ground black pepper

4 boneless, skin-on chicken breasts

1. In a small saucepan over medium heat, combine the olive oil, butter, and garlic. Cook and stir until the garlic sizzles, about 3 minutes; remove the garlic and discard.

2. Add the lemon juice, herbs, salt, and pepper to the pan. Stir and remove from heat. Let cool for 5–10 minutes. Preheat broiler.

3. Loosen the chicken skin from the flesh and pour 1 table-spoon of the lemon-herb mixture over the flesh of each breast. Smooth the skin back over the flesh.

4. Place the chicken pieces, skin-side down, on a broiler pan. Brush with the lemon mixture. Broil the chicken 4–6" from the heat source for 7–8 minutes, brushing often with the lemon mixture.

5. Turn the chicken and broil 6–9 minutes longer, brushing frequently with lemon mixture, until the chicken is thoroughly cooked. Discard any remaining lemon mixture.

6. Cut the chicken into small pieces. Serve immediately. Freeze leftovers for up to 4 weeks.

Chicken and Sun-Dried Tomatoes

Look for sun-dried tomatoes in the canned vegetable aisle at health food stores such as Whole Foods or Earth Fare.

8 SERVINGS

6 small boneless, skinless chicken thighs

¼ teaspoon ground black pepper

2 teaspoons extra-virgin olive oil

1 clove garlic, minced

½ medium yellow onion, thinly sliced

2 tablespoons sun-dried tomatoes, cut into thin strips

½ cup chicken stock (store-bought or homemade—see the recipe in Chapter 4)

2 teaspoons lemon juice

1 tablespoon chopped fresh basil

1. Rinse the chicken thighs and pat dry. Rub the pepper over the chicken.

2. Heat the olive oil in a large skillet over medium heat. Add the chicken. Cook for 5–6 minutes, until browned on both sides, turning over halfway through cooking. Stir the chicken occasionally to make sure it doesn't stick to the pan.

3. Push the chicken to the sides of the pan. Add the garlic, onion, and sun-dried tomato strips. Cook for about 3 minutes, until the onion is browned.

4. Add the chicken stock. Stir in the lemon juice. Simmer for 8–10 minutes, until the liquid is nearly absorbed and the chicken is just cooked through. Stir in the basil leaves during the last 2 minutes of cooking.

5. Cut the chicken into chewable pieces. Serve immediately. Freeze leftovers for up to 4 weeks.

Tantalizing Tandoori Chicken Remix

Tandoori chicken is a popular Indian dish traditionally marinated in a spicy yogurt mixture and baked in a tandoor oven, from which it gets its name. This recipe is a milder version of the common components of authentic tandoori chicken, but the preparation is slightly different to speed up the cooking time. You can also use boneless skinless chicken thighs if you want a juicier cut of chicken.

8 SERVINGS

¼ teaspoon ground coriander

¼ teaspoon ground cumin

¼ teaspoon ground ginger

⅛ teaspoon granulated sugar

¼ teaspoon garlic powder, or to taste

2 boneless, skinless chicken breasts, cut in half

½ cup plus 2 tablespoons full-fat plain yogurt

1 tablespoon lemon juice

1 tablespoon extra-virgin olive oil

1 clove garlic, thinly sliced

1 shallot, peeled and chopped

1. Combine the spices, sugar, and garlic powder in a small bowl. Rub over the chicken.

2. In a small bowl, combine the yogurt and lemon juice. Set aside (do not refrigerate).

3. Heat the oil in a skillet on medium-high. Add the garlic and the chicken. Pan-fry for 3–4 minutes on one side until browned.

4. Add the shallot. Turn the chicken and cook the other side until the chicken is cooked through (8–10 minutes total cooking time).

5. While the chicken is cooking, briefly heat the yogurt in a saucepan over medium heat.

6. Remove the chicken to a serving plate and spoon the yogurt mixture over the chicken. Serve immediately. Freeze leftovers for up to 4 weeks.

Perfectly Cooked Chicken Breasts
A good rule of thumb for determining when a chicken breast is done is to cook it until the meat is no longer pink or reaches an internal temperature of 165°F. Be careful not to overcook the chicken, or it may be too tough for your little one to chew and swallow.

Speedy Chicken Cordon Bleu

Traditional chicken cordon bleu is prepared by stuffing chicken breasts with ham and cheese. This toddler-friendly version is faster and easier to make but still just as delicious. Serve with steamed broccoli florets and baby carrots.

8 SERVINGS
. . . .

2 boneless, skinless chicken breasts

2 slices pancetta

½ cup whole-wheat bread crumbs
(store-bought or homemade—
see the recipe in this chapter)

2 slices baby Swiss cheese

1. Preheat oven to 400°F.

2. Pound the chicken breasts to ¼" thickness. Wrap a slice of pancetta around each chicken breast.

3. Sprinkle the bread crumbs on top of each breast and place in a 2-quart casserole dish. Bake for 10 minutes.

4. Remove the casserole from the oven, top each chicken breast with a slice of cheese, and return to the oven. Bake for 5 minutes, or until the chicken is thoroughly cooked and the cheese is melted. Serve immediately. Freeze leftovers for up to 2 weeks.

Crusty Smoky Salmon

This recipe is so good, it'll be a family favorite in no time. Save time by making the seasoned bread crumbs ahead of time. These bread crumbs can be used on any type of meat, fish, or poultry.

8 SERVINGS

1 cup cold whole milk

1 pound fresh salmon, cut into 4 fillets

1 cup whole-wheat bread crumbs
(store-bought or homemade—
see the recipe in this chapter)

½ teaspoon salt

¼ teaspoon ground black pepper

⅛ teaspoon smoked paprika

½ teaspoon garlic powder

½ teaspoon onion powder

1 teaspoon dried parsley

1 teaspoon dried dill

1. Preheat oven to 375°F. Grease a baking sheet with canola oil.

2. Soak the salmon in the cold milk for 10 minutes. Meanwhile, combine the remaining ingredients in a shallow dish.

3. Coat each salmon fillet with the bread crumb mixture (make sure to get the sides too). Place on the baking sheet.

4. Bake for 15–20 minutes, or until the salmon flakes with a fork.

5. Serve immediately. Freeze leftovers for up to 4 weeks.

Homemade Bread Crumbs

Why settle for store-bought bread crumbs when you can make your own? When you think about the cost of organic bread crumbs, it's not hard to justify a tiny bit of work. Plus, you can have fresh bread crumbs by taking just a few slices from a loaf of organic bread—and you'll save enough to buy another loaf of bread!

ABOUT 1½ CUPS
....
4 slices whole-wheat bread

1   Toast the bread in a toaster or oven for 2–3 minutes—so it is crispy but not dark. Break the bread into pieces (this will help make it all fit in the processor).

2. In a food processor, pulse the bread until it resembles fine crumbs.

3. Store in an airtight container for up to 2 weeks.

SEASONED BREAD CRUMBS

To make seasoned bread crumbs, add the following ingredients to this recipe: ½ teaspoon salt, ¼ teaspoon pepper, ⅛ teaspoon smoked paprika, ½ teaspoon garlic powder, ½ teaspoon onion powder, and 1 teaspoon dried parsley. For Italian bread crumbs, add ½ teaspoon each of oregano and basil and omit the smoked paprika.

Quick Tip: Using a Loaf of Bread
If you want to use an entire loaf of bread to make bread crumbs, cut the bread into cubes before toasting them in the oven. Then process in the food processor until fine. Use any type of bread you like.

Mozzarella Sticks

Homemade mozzarella sticks are easy to make, although you need to plan for a little freezing time required before they can be pan-fried. They can be frozen days in advance, then they'll be ready whenever you are.

8 SERVINGS
. . . .

1½ cups seasoned bread crumbs
(store-bought or homemade—
see the recipe in this chapter)

2 tablespoons grated Parmesan cheese

2 large eggs

8 sticks part-skim mozzarella cheese,
about 1" wide and 3" long

2–3 tablespoons canola oil

1. On a plate, mix together the bread crumbs and Parmesan.

2. Crack the eggs into a small bowl, and beat well.

3. Dip each stick of cheese into the beaten eggs, then into the bread crumb mixture, then back into the eggs, and one last time into the bread crumb mixture (you need lots of coating on these).

4. Place the breaded cheese in a single layer on a plate and cover with plastic wrap. Place in the freezer for at least 2 hours to freeze the cheese so it doesn't melt while cooking.

5. In large skillet, heat the oil on medium. Fry the cheese (in batches) until golden brown on each side (about 1 minute per side). Remove from the pan and drain on a paper towel.

6. Serve the cheese sticks with Marinara Sauce (Chapter 4) or Garlic Ranch Dressing (Chapter 7).

Vegetable Couscous

Couscous is a household staple in Mediterranean countries and is usually served as a side dish. Couscous is made from granules of durum wheat and is traditionally prepared by steaming.

4–6 SERVINGS

1 cup vegetable stock (store-bought or homemade—see the recipe in Chapter 4)

1 cup tricolor couscous

1½ tablespoons extra-virgin olive oil

1 clove garlic, minced

1 green onion, chopped

¼ cup peeled and shredded carrot

1 cup finely chopped broccoli florets

1. Add the stock to a small saucepan over high heat. Bring to a boil. Add the couscous. Cook for about 2 minutes, stirring occasionally. Remove from heat. Fluff with a fork.

2. Heat the olive oil in a medium skillet. Sauté the garlic, green onion, carrot, and broccoli over medium heat until the onion is softened, about 4 minutes.

3. Mix together the couscous and the vegetable mixture. Serve warm.

Fruitty Tutti Take-Along Snack

Choose your favorite brand of organic whole-wheat cereal or cereal O's for this snack. Although both of these types of cereals are great alone, they lack a serving of fruit, which this snack offers. Serve alone in a snack cup or in a bowl with milk.

10 SERVINGS

2 cups cinnamon whole-wheat cereal, such as Cascadian Farm Cinnamon Crunch Cereal

3 cups cereal O's

1 cup dried blueberries

½ cup dried strawberries

Combine all the ingredients. Store in an airtight container or bag for up to 2 weeks.

Parmesan Chicken Skillet

I love the smell of the lemon juice and thyme marinade in this dish. Serve it with Vegetable Couscous (see the recipe in this chapter) and diced cantaloupe.

12 SERVINGS
....

3 boneless, skinless chicken breasts

2 tablespoons lemon juice

¼ teaspoon salt

⅛ teaspoon ground black pepper

⅛ teaspoon dried thyme

2 tablespoons unsalted butter

½ cup grated Parmesan cheese

1. Cut the chicken breasts into ½" pieces. Transfer to a shallow bowl and sprinkle with the lemon juice, salt, pepper, and thyme. Cover and place in the refrigerator for 10 minutes.

2. Melt the butter in a heavy saucepan over medium heat. Sauté the chicken until thoroughly cooked, about 5–6 minutes, stirring frequently.

3. Sprinkle the cheese over the chicken. Turn off the heat, cover the pan, and let stand for 2–3 minutes to melt the cheese.

4. Serve over warm couscous or brown rice.

Italian Herbed Spaghetti Squash

Spaghetti squash is also known as vegetable spaghetti, as it can be used in place of pasta in most recipes. The strands are delicious tossed in olive oil, seasonings, and cheese and are especially yummy when combined with a tomato sauce, like Marinara Sauce (Chapter 4).

10 SERVINGS

1 spaghetti squash

2 tablespoons extra-virgin olive oil

1 clove garlic, minced

1 small yellow onion, chopped

1 teaspoon dried basil

1 teaspoon dried oregano

¼ cup grated Parmesan cheese (optional)

1. Preheat oven to 350°F. Cut the squash in half lengthwise and scoop out seeds.

2. Place the squash flesh side down on a lightly greased baking sheet. Bake for 30–40 minutes or until tender. Remove the squash.

3. Scrape the flesh with the tines of a fork to form spaghetti-like threads. Set aside.

4. Meanwhile, heat the olive oil in a large skillet over medium heat. Add the minced garlic, onion, and herbs. Cook for about 2 minutes, until the garlic is golden, but not brown.

5. Add the "spaghetti" squash and toss with the oil and herbs. Top with Parmesan if desired.

Orzo Pilaf

This rice-pasta combination is a winner with toddlers. The textures and different shapes are interesting to look at and feel, and the carrot adds a vegetable kick.

8 SERVINGS

1½ teaspoons extra-virgin olive oil

1 clove garlic, minced

1 small yellow onion, chopped

¼ cup pearl barley

¼ cup basmati rice

1½ cups chicken or vegetable stock (store-bought or homemade— see the recipe in Chapter 4)

⅛ teaspoon salt

¼ cup whole-wheat orzo pasta

½ cup water

¼ cup peeled and grated carrot (optional)

1. Add the olive oil, garlic, onion, and barley to a medium saucepan and sauté over medium heat for about 1 minute. Add the rice, stock, salt, orzo, and water. Bring to a boil.

2. Reduce the heat and simmer, covered, until the liquid is absorbed, about 20 minutes. Add the grated carrot if desired. Fluff with a fork. Serve. Refrigerate leftovers for up to 3 days.

Italian Snow Peas

Super quick and simple, toddlers love these crunchy snow peas. Make sure to remove all strings from the peas.

4 SERVINGS

1 tablespoon extra-virgin olive oil

1 clove garlic, minced

¾ teaspoon dried Italian seasoning

½ pound fresh snow peas, trimmed

Pinch of kosher salt

Add the olive oil to a skillet over medium heat. Stir in the garlic and Italian seasoning and cook until fragrant, about 15 seconds. Add the snow peas, tossing them in the seasoned olive oil. Cook for 1–2 minutes. Sprinkle with kosher salt. Serve.

Kale Chips

Kale has a slight bitter flavor that may not generate happy faces from the kids when you serve it to them raw. But if you dress it up with a little flavor and add some crunch, it becomes a super healthy snack that the kids can't stop eating. That's exactly the point!

4–5 SERVINGS

1 bunch fresh kale

½ tablespoon extra-virgin olive oil

1 teaspoon kosher salt

½ teaspoon garlic powder

1. Preheat oven to 375°F. Carefully tear the kale leaves from the stems and place in a colander. Wash thoroughly, making sure you wash inside any curled-up pieces.

2. Pat the leaves dry with a clean cloth or spin dry. (It's okay if a little water remains, but they should not be soaking wet.) Arrange the kale in a single layer on a baking sheet. Drizzle with the olive oil and sprinkle with the salt and garlic powder.

3. Bake for about 10 minutes, until the outer edges of the leaves turn brown. Remove from the oven. The leaves will crisp more as they stand. Serve immediately. Store in an airtight container and consume within 2 days.

Farmers' Market Kale

Visit your local farmers' market for great prices on organic kale. Although many small farms are not regulated by the USDA, you can talk directly to the farmers about the use of pesticides in their produce.

Grape Streusel Bars

These soft bars are perfect for a healthy snack. Make sure the grapes you use don't contain any seeds before adding them. Sometimes seedless varieties will have a few seed surprises, so it's always good to double-check.

16 SERVINGS

1 cup unbleached all-purpose flour

½ cup quick-cooking oats

½ cup light brown sugar

⅛ teaspoon ground allspice

⅓ cup unsalted butter, melted

1 cup chopped red seedless grapes

2 tablespoons grape jelly

1. Preheat oven to 350°F. In a large bowl, combine the flour, oats, brown sugar, and allspice and mix well. Add the melted butter and stir until the mixture forms crumbs. Press half of the crumbs into a 9" × 9" pan and set aside.

2. In a small bowl, combine the grapes and jelly and mix well. Spoon over the crust in the pan and spread out evenly. Sprinkle the top with the remaining crumb mixture.

3. Bake for 15–20 minutes, or until the bars are light golden brown. Let cool and cut into bars.

Table Grapes

Many grapes currently sold in produce departments are seedless. They are called "table grapes" to distinguish them from grapes used to make wine. You can buy red, green, or blue-black grapes. Varieties include Flame, Thompson Seedless, Red Globe, Autumn Royal, and Christmas Rose.

Triple-Berry Blastoff

Triple the berries for triple the antioxidants, triple the vitamins, and triple the delicious flavor. Including romaine lettuce gives your toddler almost 100 percent of his vitamin K intake for the day.

4 SERVINGS

1 cup roughly chopped romaine lettuce

1 pint blueberries

1 pint raspberries

2 pints strawberries

2 bananas

1 cup whole milk

1 cup Greek vanilla yogurt

1. Add the lettuce, blueberries, raspberries, strawberries, bananas, and milk to a blender and blend until smooth.

2. Add the yogurt and blend until thoroughly mixed. Serve immediately.

Freeze Your Own Strawberries

When strawberries are in season, cash in on the savings and stock up on the berries. The best deals can be found at your local farmers' market, where you can get large quantities for a low price, or head over to a "pick your own" farm. Then, have a strawberry-freezing party and invite the family over to help. To freeze, cut the stems out of unwashed strawberries. Make sure the strawberries are completely dry. Lay them on a wax paper–lined cookie sheet and freeze them for 2–4 hours, until they begin to firm up. This way the strawberries will freeze separately and not in one big clump. Then, scoop all the strawberries into a freezer-safe bag for storing in the freezer. They will last 10–12 months, but don't forget to rinse them off before you use them.

Purple Cow on the Rocks

Instead of resorting to juice, offer milk blends like this one, which offers a serving of dairy, fruit, and protein. If your child can't tolerate dairy, feel free to use an alternative milk such as soy or coconut milk.

2 SERVINGS

1½ cups ice cubes

⅔ cup frozen blueberries and strawberries

⅔ cup whole milk

Add all the ingredients to a blender. Blend until smooth, about 30 seconds. Serve immediately.

The Scoop on Vitamin D

Vitamin D helps your body absorb calcium by moving calcium from your intestines into your bloodstream and bones. Cow's milk is often fortified with vitamin D, but you can also get vitamin D through safe sun exposure (three times a week for about 10–15 minutes without sunscreen). Children from birth to 18 years need 400 IU of vitamin D per day.

American Dream Potato Salad

Potato salad is a good meal to take to spring and summer cookouts or potlucks. There's no need to heat it up; just pop it in a container with an ice pack and serve within a few hours. The eggs provide protein, so it makes a great snack for toddlers, especially with a piece of whole-wheat toast.

8 SERVINGS

2 large russet potatoes, peeled and cut into small cubes

2 hard-boiled eggs, finely chopped

½ medium red onion, chopped

½ stalk celery, finely chopped

2 tablespoons prepared yellow mustard

½ cup mayonnaise

2 tablespoons sweet relish

½ teaspoon salt, or to taste

¼ teaspoon ground black pepper, or to taste

¼ teaspoon paprika

1. Place the potatoes in a medium pot with enough cold water to cover. Bring to a boil over high heat. Reduce heat to medium-low, cover, and simmer until fork-tender, about 15 minutes. Drain and set aside to cool completely.

2. In a large bowl, mix the cooled potatoes with the remaining ingredients. Serve immediately or cover and chill for 1–2 hours and serve cold. Refrigerate leftovers for up to 3 days.

Double Melon Quencher

This smoothie delivers ultimate hydration and nutrition for toddlers on hot summer days. Plain ice water is an excellent choice, but it doesn't offer the calories and nutrition needed for a boost of energy to climb at the playground. This recipe gives plain water an upgrade!

4 SERVINGS

1 cup roughly chopped romaine lettuce

2 cups chopped seedless watermelon

2 cups chopped cantaloupe

½ lemon, peeled

½ lime, peeled

2 cups water

1. Combine the romaine, watermelon, cantaloupe, lemon, lime, and 1 cup water in a blender and blend for about 30 seconds.

2. Add the remaining 1 cup water and blend to desired consistency. Serve immediately.

> *Save Your Rinds—They Make Awesome Serving Dishes!*
> You don't need to toss the watermelon rind after you cut it—recycle it into a serving dish. Cut the watermelon in half across the middle and use a melon baller to scoop out the flesh. (Keep the rind intact.) Then add a variety of melons, strawberries, blueberries, and chopped pineapple to the "bowl." Grate ginger over the top and stir. Your watermelon bowl fruit salad makes a beautiful and fun centerpiece.

Cherry Potion

There's so much fruit in this drink, your toddler won't even realize there is spinach in the mix too. Cherries are known for improving sleep, so when your child is restless try this cherry potion and see if it magically induces a nap!

4 SERVINGS

1 cup spinach

2 cups pitted Bing cherries

1 Gala apple, cored and peeled

1 teaspoon pure vanilla extract

2 cups water

1. Combine the spinach, cherries, apple, vanilla extract, and 1 cup water in a blender. Blend until smooth.

2. Add the remaining 1 cup water and blend again until all ingredients are well incorporated. Serve immediately.

How to Pit a Cherry

If you don't have a cherry pitter, use a drinking straw to poke a hole in one end and push it all the way through to remove the pit from the other end. Another way is to use a cake-decorating tip (or pastry tip) in the same manner (it's a little sturdier).

Pizza Burger Dogs

Here's a cool twist on a traditional hot dog. This loose burger/dog contains a nice serving of vegetables and whole grains. Serve with a small salad.

8 SERVINGS

1 pound lean ground beef
or ground chicken

½ small yellow onion, chopped

2 cloves garlic, minced

½ teaspoon kosher salt

½ teaspoon dried Italian seasoning

⅓ cup pizza sauce (store-bought or homemade—see the recipe in Chapter 7)

8 whole-wheat hot dog buns

½ cup shredded mozzarella cheese

1. Add the ground beef or chicken to a large skillet over medium-high heat. Add the onion, garlic, salt, and Italian seasoning. Mix well. Cook until the meat is no longer pink, about 8–10 minutes. Drain off excess fat.

2. Add the pizza sauce to the pan and stir to mix. Cook for about 2 minutes, until heated through.

3. Scoop a couple tablespoons of the meat mixture into each hot dog bun. Top with shredded mozzarella cheese. Serve immediately.

Berry Fruity Cobb Salad

Serving leafy greens with at least two meals per day is essential for laying the foundation of a healthy palate. Although this salad includes a lot of nutrient-rich fruit, romaine lettuce certainly has a presence and provides plant-based vitamins and minerals that keep our bodies healthy.

2 SERVINGS

½ cup coarsely chopped romaine lettuce

6 mandarin orange segments, cut in half

4 Gala apple slices, cut into small cubes

3 whole strawberries, hulled and cut into bite-size pieces

¼ ripe avocado, cut into small cubes

¼ cup cubed smoked turkey breast

Florida Orange Yogurt Dressing, to taste (see the recipe in this chapter)

1. Arrange the lettuce on a small plate.

2. Arrange the oranges, apples, strawberries, avocado, and turkey breast on top of lettuce in rows.

3. Drizzle the dressing over the salad. Serve immediately.

Florida Orange Yogurt Dressing

My husband and I were on our honeymoon when I first tasted orange salad dressing. Now we eat it with our kids, who always eat their greens when this salad dressing is poured on. Try it on any salad. It's sweet without overpowering the salad.

8 SERVINGS

¼ cup orange juice

½ cup plain Greek yogurt

¼ cup sour cream

2 tablespoons honey

2 teaspoons white wine vinegar

Whisk together all the ingredients until smooth. Refrigerate until ready to serve. Can be refrigerated for up to 5 days.

Pear Vinaigrette Dressing

Serve this wonderful Pear Vinaigrette Dressing with a simple garden salad consisting of chopped romaine, cucumber, and shredded carrots for a quick and easy side dish.

8 SERVINGS

1 ripe Bartlett pear, peeled, cored, and chopped

¼ cup apple cider vinegar

2 teaspoons prepared yellow mustard

⅛ teaspoon salt

⅛ teaspoon ground black pepper

½ cup extra-virgin olive oil

Blend the pear, vinegar, mustard, salt, and pepper in a blender for about 30 seconds while gradually pouring in the olive oil. Refrigerate for up to 1 week.

Change Up the Dressings
Mix and match salad dressings when your toddler seems to get bored eating the same salad with the same dressings. For example, pair the Chopped Strawberry Fields Salad with Pear Vinaigrette Dressing or the Berry Fruity Cobb Salad with Raspberry Vinaigrette Dressing (see this chapter for recipes).

Chopped Strawberry Fields Salad

Be sure you cut the greens nice and small so they fit in toddlers' little mouths. This salad is a nice way to introduce a new green—with the fresh fruit and a sweet salad dressing, she might not mind!

2 SERVINGS

¼ cup roughly chopped romaine lettuce

¼ cup roughly chopped baby spinach

¼ cup roughly chopped kale

5 strawberries, chopped

2 tablespoons diced fresh peaches

1 tablespoon feta cheese

Raspberry Vinaigrette Dressing, to taste (see the recipe in this chapter)

1. Combine the romaine, spinach, and kale.

2. Top with the strawberries, peaches, and feta cheese.

3. Drizzle individual servings of the salad with the dressing. Serve immediately. Refrigerate leftover salad for 2–3 days (without the dressing).

Surprise Chicken Nuggets

Ground chicken makes these nuggets super easy to prepare and bake. There is no need to stop by any drive-through when you can make organic chicken nuggets free of all the yucky additives. These nuggets have surprise grated carrot to throw in some beta-carotene to the mix.

8 SERVINGS

1 cup whole-wheat bread crumbs (store-bought or homemade— see the recipe in this chapter)

½ teaspoon garlic powder

½ teaspoon onion powder

1 pound ground chicken

¼ cup peeled and grated carrot

¼ teaspoon ground black pepper

¼ teaspoon paprika

¼ teaspoon salt

1. Preheat oven to 375°F. Lightly grease a nonstick baking sheet with extra-virgin olive oil. Add the bread crumbs, garlic powder, and onion powder to a shallow dish. Stir to combine. Set aside.

2. In a large bowl, mix the chicken with the carrot. Stir in the pepper, paprika, and salt. Moisten your hands with water or oil to prevent sticking and shape the chicken into 2" balls, then press them flat with your fingers.

3. Press the nuggets into the bread mixture. Coat on both sides. Arrange in the prepared baking dish.

4. Bake for 15 minutes or until lightly browned, turning once halfway through the baking time. Freeze leftovers for up to 4 weeks.

Raspberry Vinaigrette Dressing

A flavorful salad dressing is key to getting your child to love salads. I've found that fruity salad dressings go over very well in training the little ones to learn to love greens, especially when made with a fruit they already love. If the salad dressing is good, the greens will get eaten along with it.

8 SERVINGS

1 cup fresh raspberries

¼ cup apple cider vinegar

½ cup extra-virgin olive oil

2 tablespoons honey

Combine all the ingredients in a blender and mix until smooth. Serve. Refrigerate for up to 1 week.

Peach Grape Crush

Whole fruit offers a lot more nutrition than fruit juice. This recipe uses grapes and peaches, skins and all, to create this slushy drink.

4 SERVINGS

1 cup frozen peaches

1 cup green seedless grapes

½ cup lemon juice

¼ cup honey

1 cup ice

Combine all the ingredients in a blender. Blend for 30 seconds. Serve immediately.

Fruit-Infused Milk

When I was a little girl, I only drank flavored milk made from a powdered mix. Even though my kids love milk as it is, I still have a secret aversion to it unless it's flavored. Now that I'm older and wiser, I flavor my milk naturally with fruit. If your child is not a milk lover, try infusing it with fruit.

8 SERVINGS
· · · · · · · · · · · · ·

½ banana

10 large strawberries, hulled

¼ cup raspberries

4 cups whole milk or coconut milk

1. Slice the banana and strawberries. Cut the raspberries in half.

2. Add all the ingredients to a pitcher and stir to combine. Refrigerate overnight to allow the flavors to develop (or chill for 4 hours if your child can't wait).

3. Strain the fruit from the milk. Consume within 2 days of infusing.

Try Flavored Cereal
Not only can you serve your child Fruit-Infused Milk straight from a cup, but you can also add it to her breakfast cereal (fruit and all) for additional nutrients and flavor.

Three-Bean Salad

It's important to prepare this salad the day before you want to serve it, because it has to marinate in the refrigerator for the beans to absorb the dressing and develop the flavors. It's definitely worth the wait.

6 SERVINGS

¼ cup extra-virgin olive oil

⅓ cup apple cider vinegar

½ teaspoon dry mustard

½ teaspoon salt, or to taste

⅛ teaspoon ground black pepper, or to taste

¼ cup minced red onion

1 large clove garlic, minced

1 tablespoon honey

1 (15-ounce) can green beans, drained and rinsed

1 (15-ounce) can kidney beans, drained and rinsed

1 (15-ounce) can garbanzo beans (chickpeas), drained and rinsed

1. In a small bowl, whisk together the olive oil, vinegar, mustard, salt, pepper, and onion.

2. Place all the beans in a salad bowl, add the dressing, and toss gently to coat the beans. Cover and refrigerate overnight before serving. Refrigerate leftovers for up to 3 days.

Honey Mustard Salmon

Honey mustard dressing makes an irresistible marinade for salmon. Grill outside or broil in the oven—your choice. Serve on a bed of baby spinach.

8 SERVINGS
••••••••••••••

⅓ cup Honey Mustard Dressing
(see the recipe in Chapter 7)

½ teaspoon dried dill

2 tablespoons unsalted butter, melted

4 (4-ounce) salmon fillets

1. In a shallow casserole dish, combine the salad dressing, dill, and butter and mix well. Add the salmon fillets and turn to coat. Refrigerate for 10 minutes.

2. Preheat grill or broiler. Remove the salmon from the marinade and place skin-side down on the grill or broiler pan. Grill or broil 6" from the heat source for 8–12 minutes, until the salmon flakes easily with a fork. Brush with the remaining marinade halfway through cooking time. (Discard any unused marinade.) Serve immediately.

Smothered Asparagus

Medium-size stalks of asparagus work best for this recipe. Sautéing them in the oil makes them tender with a little crunch for toddlers to eat, and also offers a nice serving of healthy fat.

4 SERVINGS

2 tablespoons extra-virgin olive oil

1 clove garlic, minced

5 asparagus spears

½ teaspoon kosher salt

Pinch of ground black pepper

2 tablespoons grated Parmesan cheese

1. Preheat the oil in a medium skillet over medium heat. Sauté the garlic for 30 seconds. Add the asparagus and toss with the oil to coat. Cook until tender, about 7 minutes.

2. Season with salt and pepper. Sprinkle the Parmesan over the top. Cover to melt cheese. Serve immediately.

The Power of Asparagus

Asparagus helps fight free radicals in the body and may protect against bone, breast, lung, and colon cancer—and it's also known to help destroy carcinogens. It provides a large dose of folic acid and is a great source of fiber, magnesium, calcium, potassium, and vitamins A, B_6, C, and K.

Coconut Teriyaki Shrimp

Another winner in my house, both kids and adults love this recipe. Serve over warm brown rice with a side of steamed broccoli and Grilled Pineapple (Chapter 6).

4 SERVINGS

1 pound large domestic shrimp, shelled, deveined, tail on

½ teaspoon salt

1 cup non-GMO cornstarch, or more as needed for coating

¼ cup coconut oil

⅓ cup Honey Teriyaki Sauce (see the recipe in Chapter 7)

1. Remove the tails from the shrimp.

2. Place the shrimp in a bowl and toss with the salt. Coat the shrimp thoroughly with cornstarch.

3. Heat the coconut oil in a large skillet over medium-high heat. Once the oil is hot, add the shrimp. Cook both sides until crispy (it's okay if the coating looks pale), about 2 minutes on each side. Remove the shrimp from the pan. Wipe the pan clean. Place the pan back on the stove over medium-high heat.

4. Add the shrimp to the warm pan. Pour the teriyaki sauce over the shrimp. Cook for an additional minute. Serve immediately.

Tex-Mex Fried Rice

This highly seasoned rice provides a good balance of spice when served with lightly seasoned chicken breast or beef.

16 SERVINGS
. . . .

3 tablespoons vegetable oil, divided

½ medium yellow onion, finely chopped

1 tomato, diced

1 cup fresh corn kernels

3 cups cooked long-grain white rice, cold

½ teaspoon ground cumin

2 green onions, finely sliced

¼ teaspoon salt, or to taste

⅛ teaspoon ground black pepper, or to taste

1. Heat 1½ tablespoons of the oil in a nonstick skillet over medium heat. Add the onion. Cook for 4–5 minutes, until the onion is softened.

2. Stir in the tomato. Cook for 1 minute. Stir in the corn. Transfer the vegetables to a bowl and set aside.

3. Heat the remaining oil in the pan. Add the rice. Cook, stirring, for 1–2 minutes, until heated through. Stir in the cumin.

4. Return the vegetables to the pan. Add the green onions. Stir to mix everything together. Season with the salt and pepper. Serve hot.

Tofu Avocado Spread

Rich in protein, iron, and potassium, this creamy spread serves nicely atop a piece of whole-grain toast. Avocados offer a healthy serving of monounsaturated fat that your toddler needs for healthy brain development.

½ CUP
••••••••

¼ cup firm tofu

½ ripe avocado

1 teaspoon lemon juice

1 clove garlic, minced

½ Roma tomato, seeded
and finely chopped

1. Combine the tofu, avocado, lemon juice, and garlic in a blender or food processor. Blend until smooth.

2. Transfer the mixture to a bowl and fold in the tomatoes. Store in the refrigerator for up to 3 days.

Ambrosia Yogurt Cup

Many toddlers love the taste of coconut. You can purchase organic coconut flakes and toast a larger batch to keep on hand. Then, take out what you need for this recipe and use whatever is leftover to add to other recipes in this book, like Cinnamon Granola Crunch Cereal (Chapter 7).

1 SERVING

¼ cup chopped, canned mandarin oranges

½ cup Greek vanilla yogurt

1 heaping tablespoon coconut flakes, toasted (see sidebar)

Layer in this order: ¼ cup yogurt, orange sections, remaining ¼ cup yogurt. Top with coconut.

Five-Minute Toasted Coconut

Pour coconut flakes in a large skillet and cook over medium-high heat, stirring frequently until the flakes are golden brown. Store in an airtight container for up to 2 weeks.

Happy Birthday Melon "Cake"

This easy melon "cake" is so fast to make because it doesn't require any time baking in the oven. A healthier alternative to traditional birthday cake, the vibrant colors of fruit will entice any toddler.

12 SERVINGS

1 personal-size watermelon or
½ medium-size watermelon

3 cups whipped cream (store-bought or homemade—see the recipe in this chapter), optional

3 small kiwifruit, peeled and sliced

2 nectarines, peeled and sliced

1 pint strawberries, hulled and halved

1. Slice the watermelon into rounds about 1" thick. Carefully cut away the rind, being careful to maintain the circle shape.

2. On a cake platter, layer the watermelon circles with the whipped cream, if using. If not, stack the watermelon circles. For a tiered look, trim each circle about 2" smaller than the previous layer (eat the leftover as you cut away—we don't want that juicy watermelon to go to waste!).

3. Arrange the kiwifruit, nectarines, and strawberries on top of the watermelon any way you choose. Be creative!

Make It Personal
Personal-size watermelons are perfect for making this beautiful watermelon cake for your child's birthday. For a more elaborate cake, grab a bigger watermelon that can serve a large crowd. Watermelon is known to have little to no traces of pesticides, so if you can't find an organic watermelon, it's safe for toddlers to eat—no worries.

Homemade Maple Whipped Cream

This is my go-to recipe whenever I need whipped cream. It's important to keep everything chilled for the mixture to whip properly, so place all the ingredients in the freezer for about 7 minutes prior to whipping. The results are fantastic! Use this recipe to top off any dessert.

ABOUT 3 CUPS

1 pint heavy whipping cream

3 tablespoons pure maple syrup

1 teaspoon pure vanilla extract

1. Beat the cream in a large bowl (using a stand or hand mixer) on a medium setting until soft peaks begin to form.

2. Gradually incorporate the maple syrup and vanilla and beat until stiff peaks form. Use immediately or refrigerate for up to 24 hours.

Whip It to Perfection

As soon as the stiff peaks form (meaning it stands in straight, firm peaks on a spoon or whipping attachments), stop whipping. Overwhipping may cause the mixture to separate after being stored in the refrigerator. If this happens, don't throw it out! It's still good to use. Rewhip by hand using a whisk or use a stand or hand mixer to revive.

Frozen Raspberry Ice

This is a healthy version of a similar icy treat with no added sugar or artificial colors. It still delivers a bright color that many kids love, but naturally.

4 SERVINGS

2 cups raspberries

1 teaspoon pure vanilla extract

3 tablespoons frozen apple juice concentrate

1. Combine all the ingredients in a blender. Blend until smooth, about 30 seconds.

2. Press the mixture through a fine-mesh sieve to remove the seeds. Pour the mixture into a freezer-safe container.

3. Freeze for 2 hours, then fluff with a fork. Return to freezer. Repeat this step one more time.

4. Serve fluffed.

CHAPTER 6
THE PICKY EATER—
18 TO 24 MONTHS

As your child approaches 24 months, you may notice a shift in his eating habits. He suddenly tosses those sweet potatoes he used to gobble up. Suddenly, he no longer likes sauce on his pasta. This can be a trying time for parents because you wonder if your toddler is getting enough nutrition from the few kernels of corn he chose to eat today. Or, you worry why she doesn't seem to have an appetite after many hours of playing, and mealtime becomes a battle where she throws food on the floor instead of eating it.

Around this time, the 1-year growth spurt has come and gone and growth is slow and steady. You may notice a whole new attitude around food, especially when it comes to colors and textures. However, remain consistent, offering varied, well-balanced meals, and continue to persevere and pair foods you know he likes with a new food.

On the plus side: You may also find that suddenly he likes mashed potatoes, while he refused them as an infant. So, break out the foods he didn't seem to care for during the earlier months and see if he likes them now!

IMPORTANT TIPS TO REMEMBER FOR THE PICKY EATER

- Your toddler is likely to still graze—eating small amounts of food all day long. Therefore, keep plenty of foods readily available from each food group for snacking. You may find by the end of the day, although she didn't sit down to a traditional meal, the grazing was substantial enough to meet her nutritional requirements.
- Minimize distractions during mealtimes. No television during meals.
- Allow your toddler to help cook meals in the kitchen to help develop an appreciation for food, and encourage eating it.
- Be sensitive to new teeth that are still emerging. If your toddler is not eating as she normally does, it could be that new molars are coming through. If this is the case, chilled soups are a baby's best friend.
- Offer your child a small meal or snack every 2–3 hours, and don't stress if he doesn't eat it all.
- Share! Toddlers often want what their parents are eating, so carve out a section of food on your plate for your toddler to munch.

Egg and Cheese Strata

Stratas are great to whip together the night before a holiday or special occasion (or when you want to sleep in and not worry about spending time making breakfast). Add vegetables you may have on hand, like mushrooms or spinach, for a nutritional boost.

16 SERVINGS

¼ cup unsalted butter

6 slices whole-wheat bread

1 cup shredded Cheddar cheese

6 large eggs

1 cup whole milk

½ cup mashed cooked butternut squash

¼ teaspoon Dijon mustard

1. Butter the bread and cut into 1" cubes.

2. In a medium bowl, combine the bread and cheese. Transfer to a lightly greased 9" pie dish.

3. Whisk together the eggs, whole milk, butternut squash, and mustard. Pour the mixture over the bread and cheese. Cover and refrigerate overnight.

4. Preheat oven to 375°F. Uncover the strata and bake for 20–30 minutes or until the top is brown and bubbly. Serve immediately. Refrigerate leftovers for up to 3 days.

Black Bean Breakfast Burrito

This burrito boasts protein, fiber, and whole grains as a healthy way for your toddler to start her busy day. The rolled-up burrito might be fun for her to play with, too—as long as she gets the food in her mouth eventually, don't worry about it!

2 SERVINGS

¼ cup canned black beans, drained

2 large eggs

1 tablespoon whole milk

¼ cup mild shredded Cheddar cheese

1 (6") whole-wheat flour tortilla

Salsa (store-bought or homemade—see the recipe in this chapter), to taste

1. In a small saucepan over medium heat, cook the black beans until hot. Mash with a fork.

2. In a small bowl, whisk together the eggs and milk.

3. Add the egg mixture and cheese to a small skillet over medium heat and scramble until cooked to desired doneness.

4. Spread the tortilla with a thin layer of the mashed black beans and salsa. Top with the scrambled eggs.

5. Roll up the tortilla. Cut in half. Refrigerate leftovers for up to 2 days.

Homemade Toaster Pastries

This recipe is a little labor intensive, but certainly worth the effort. Instead of the cardboard toaster pastries we had as kids, this version provides fresh flavors (without the additives) and the fragrant smell of grandma's home-baked pies. They are treats, though, so serve them sparingly.

6 SERVINGS

1¼ cups whole-wheat flour

1¼ cups unbleached all-purpose flour, plus more for rolling

1 teaspoon salt

2 sticks (1 cup) cold unsalted butter

⅓ cup ice-cold water

1 large egg

6 tablespoons fruit preserves

1. In the bowl of a food processor, combine the flours and salt. Cut the cold butter into ½" cubes. Scatter the butter around the bowl. Place the bowl of flour and butter in the freezer for 10 minutes (this will help ensure the mixture stays cold).

2. Remove the bowl from the freezer and pulse the mixture until crumbly. Using the feed tube, slowly pour in the ice-cold water until blended, about 10–20 seconds. At this point the mixture should no longer be crumbly, but more doughy. Remove the dough from the bowl and divide in half. Quickly shape into 2 disks. Wrap each disk in wax paper and refrigerate for at least 45 minutes or up to 2 days.

3. Preheat oven to 375°F. Remove the dough from the refrigerator. Let stand on the counter for about 10–15 minutes or until pliable enough to roll out. Meanwhile, line a large baking sheet with parchment paper or silicone liner. Beat the egg with 1 tablespoon of water. Set aside. Lightly flour a clean surface.

4. Roll out each dough disk with a rolling pin into a 9" × 12" rectangle (use a ruler!). Cut away jagged edges with a knife. Cut 6 (3" × 4") rectangles from each disk.

CONTINUED ON NEXT PAGE

5. Spread 1 tablespoon of the fruit preserves in the center of 6 of the rectangles. Top with the remaining rectangles. Press the sides together with a fork. Brush each pastry with the egg mixture. Poke a few rows of holes into the top of the pastries with a fork.

6. Bakes for 25–30 minutes or until golden brown. Remove promptly and allow to cool for 15 minutes before serving. Freeze remaining pastries for up to 4 weeks.

Fillings for Toaster Pastries

From sweet to savory, you can use anything to fill homemade toaster pastries. Any type of fruit preserves will work to make sweet versions. To make savory pastries, try adding sweet potatoes or marinara sauce and shredded cheese.

Apple Orchard Muffins

Apples provide a great source of fiber and research shows that apple polyphenols can help prevent blood sugar spikes. Mix them up in this muffin for a nutritious snack after you and your toddler have picked apples in the fall.

12 SERVINGS

1 large egg

½ cup orange juice

¼ cup canola oil

1½ cups Gala or Granny Smith apples, peeled and diced

1½ cups unbleached all-purpose flour

½ cup granulated sugar

2 teaspoons baking powder

TOPPING

1 teaspoon ground cinnamon

¼ cup light brown sugar

1. Preheat oven to 400°F. Spray a 12-cup muffin pan with nonstick cooking spray, or insert baking cups.

2. Combine the egg, orange juice, canola oil, apples, flour, sugar, and baking powder in a large mixing bowl. Mix until well blended.

3. Pour the batter into the prepared pan.

4. Prepare the topping in a small bowl by combining the cinnamon and brown sugar. Sprinkle the topping over each muffin.

5. Bake for 20–25 minutes, until a toothpick inserted into the center of a muffin comes out clean. Freeze for up to 2 weeks.

Belgian Waffle Wedges

I keep a Belgian waffle iron (the kind that flips) on my countertop to make waffles at a moment's notice. You can serve them any time of day, and they're great snacks for toddlers because the topping choices are endless. Try fresh berries, bananas, jam, a few mini chocolate chips, or maple syrup.

16–20 SERVINGS

1 cup whole-wheat flour

1 cup unbleached all-purpose flour

3 teaspoons baking powder

3 tablespoons turbinado
or granulated sugar

½ cup coconut oil

2 cups 2% milk

2 large eggs

1 teaspoon pure vanilla extract

½ teaspoon salt

1. Preheat a Belgian waffle iron and grease each well with oil or cooking spray. Combine all the ingredients in a large bowl. Mix well.

2. To make each waffle, pour about ½ to 1 cup of batter (more or less depending on the size iron) into the hot waffle iron. Spread into the wells with a spatula.

3. Cook for about 2–3 minutes or until crisp golden brown.

4. Cut the waffles into quarters (wedges). Top each wedge with fruit or your favorite topping and serve. Freeze leftovers for up to 4 weeks.

Perfect Pairings
Add a serving of protein (e.g., scrambled eggs or ham), low-fat cottage cheese, or a glass of milk for a fast and complete breakfast.

Berrylicious Smoothie

This recipe offers seven powerful superfoods in one sip. Each of the berries contains an abundance of antioxidants alone, so just think of the power of three of them combined. Coupled with the green power of spinach, the immune support from the clementines, the potassium from the bananas, and the calcium from the milk, don't be surprised if you see your toddler flying tomorrow!

4 SERVINGS

1 cup spinach

1 banana

1 cup strawberries

1 cup blueberries

1 cup blackberries

2 clementines or tangerines, sectioned

1 cup whole milk

1. Combine the spinach, banana, strawberries, blueberries, blackberries, clementines, and ½ cup milk in a high-powered blender and blend.

2. Continue to blend and add the remaining ½ cup milk until smooth. Serve immediately.

Breakfast Crepes

Crepes are similar to pancakes, but they are lighter, thinner, and traditionally prepared with fruit fillings such as Skillet Apples (Chapter 4), or something simple like strawberries and yogurt.

8 SERVINGS

1 cup unbleached all-purpose flour, sifted

1 large egg

1 egg yolk

1 cup nonfat milk

⅛ teaspoon salt

2 tablespoons unsalted butter, melted

1–2 tablespoons coconut oil or canola oil

1. In a large bowl, whisk all the ingredients together until smooth.

2. Heat a lightly oiled skillet over medium-high heat. Pour the batter into the pan, using approximately ¼ cup for each crepe. Tilt the pan in a circular motion to coat the surface evenly. Cook for about 2 minutes, or until the bottom is golden. Turn using a spatula, and cook the other side until golden. Repeat with the remaining batter.

3. Fill with your favorite filling, roll, and serve. Refrigerate crepes without filling for up to 3 days.

Versatile Crepes

Use the crepe recipe on this page as a base for any filling your toddler might enjoy. Crepe fillings can consists of any combination of foods. If he likes crepes, use the filling to introduce new flavors you want him to try—just fill, roll, and watch him eat!

Sautéed Cabbage

I've found the most beautiful cabbage heads at the farmers' market, with large vibrant green outer leaves. Sometimes, when you purchase cabbage at the store, the outer leaves get destroyed in the shipping process and you're often left with only the white part of the cabbage. For the best results, buy a cabbage with all the leaves intact.

6 SERVINGS

½ small head green cabbage, cored

3 tablespoons extra-virgin olive oil

1 teaspoon kosher salt

½ teaspoon ground black pepper

1. Cut the cabbage into thin slices lengthwise.

2. Heat the oil in a large skillet over medium-high heat. Add the cabbage, tossing to coat.

3. Season with the salt and pepper and cook, stirring occasionally, for about 15–20 minutes, until tender. Serve.

Apple Lemonade Sipper

Summertime and lemonade go hand in hand, but prepared lemonade can contain more sugar than you would like your toddler to have. Instead, make your own fresh lemonade so you control the sweetener.

4 SERVINGS

2 Gala apples, peeled and cored

2 cups freshly squeezed lemon juice

1 tablespoon honey

2 cups water

1 cup ice

1. Combine the apple, lemon juice, honey, and 1 cup water in a blender and blend for 30 seconds.

2. Add the remaining water and the ice and blend until smooth and thoroughly mixed. Serve immediately.

Summer Turkey Tenderloin

The best part of summer is being able to grill outside. This turkey tenderloin is one of the first things you can make in celebration of the new season. Serve it with Smothered Asparagus (Chapter 5) or Broccoli Parmesan (see the recipe in this chapter).

8 SERVINGS

1 pound turkey tenderloin

½ cup orange juice

2 tablespoons Dijon mustard

¼ cup honey

2 cloves garlic

½ teaspoon salt

⅛ teaspoon ground black pepper

1. Preheat grill on medium. Butterfly the tenderloin by cutting it in half lengthwise, being careful not to cut all the way through (stop about 1" from the other side). Spread the tenderloin open, cover it with plastic wrap, and pound gently with a meat mallet or rolling pin to flatten.

2. Combine the remaining ingredients in a large resealable plastic bag. Add the turkey. Close the bag and knead it, pressing the marinade into the turkey. Let stand at room temperature for 10 minutes.

3. Grill the turkey about 6" from the heat source for 5 minutes, brushing it with any leftover marinade. Turn the turkey and cook for 4–6 minutes, until no longer pink inside. Discard any remaining marinade. Serve immediately. Freeze leftovers for up to 2 weeks.

Crispy Honey Chicken Nuggets

These chicken nuggets are bite-size but so they are much healthier than the takeout version. Serve this dish with a side of brown rice and Sautéed Cabbage (see the recipe in this chapter).

4 SERVINGS
. . . .

1 pound boneless, skinless chicken breast, cut into 1" chunks

2 teaspoons salt

1 cup non-GMO cornstarch, or more as needed for coating

Canola oil, for frying

GINGER HONEY SAUCE

1 tablespoon non-GMO cornstarch

1 tablespoon water

½ cup honey

1 tablespoon rice wine vinegar

2 tablespoons tamari soy sauce (low-sodium)

¼ teaspoon ground ginger

1. Place the chicken in a bowl and toss with the salt. Coat the chicken thoroughly with cornstarch.

2. To make the sauce, whisk together all the ingredients.

3. Add ½" oil to a large skillet over medium-high heat. Once hot, add the chicken. Cook until crispy (it's okay if the coating looks pale), about 2 minutes on each side. Remove the chicken from the pan. Wipe the pan clean. Place the pan back on the stove over medium-high heat.

4. Add the chicken nuggets to the warm pan. Pour the prepared sauce over the chicken. Stir to coat. Cook for an additional minute. Serve immediately. Can be frozen for up to 2 weeks.

Grilled Turkey Sliders

All the spices make these sliders very flavorful. Add a few baby spinach leaves on the sliders for the grand finale presentation (and some iron). Serve with a side of fruit.

8 SERVINGS

½ cup whole-wheat bread crumbs
(store-bought or homemade—
see the recipe in Chapter 5)

1 large egg, beaten

½ teaspoon salt

¼ teaspoon ground black pepper

½ teaspoon onion powder

¼ teaspoon ground cumin

1 teaspoon chili powder

1 pound ground turkey

8 slices provolone cheese

8 whole-wheat rolls, split in half

1. Preheat grill on medium. In a large bowl, combine the bread crumbs, egg, salt, pepper, cumin, and chili powder and mix well. Add the turkey and mix gently but thoroughly until combined. Form into 8 small patties, about 3" in diameter.

2. Cook the patties 4–6" from the heat source for about 10 minutes, turning once, until thoroughly cooked (cook with the grill cover closed). Top each with a slice of cheese, cover, and cook for 1 minute longer, until the cheese melts. Meanwhile, toast the rolls cut-side down.

3. Make sandwiches with the turkey patties and buns. Serve hot.

Shrimp Linguine

Shrimp is high in protein and omega-3 fatty acids and a favorite seafood for many toddlers. However, make sure the vein is removed from the shrimp before you prepare it.

4–6 SERVINGS

8 ounces linguine

4 slices thick-cut bacon

1 pound large domestic shrimp, peeled, deveined, and tail removed

2 tablespoons unsalted butter

1 cup half-and-half

½ cup grated Parmesan cheese

½ teaspoon salt

¼ teaspoon ground black pepper

1. Bring a large pot of water to a boil and cook the linguine according to package directions.

2. Meanwhile, heat a large skillet over medium-high heat. Cook the bacon until crisp and transfer to a paper towel. Drain all but about 1 tablespoon of bacon fat from the pan.

3. Return the pan to the stove. Over medium-high heat, cook the shrimp in the bacon fat (or olive oil, if preferred) until pink. Remove from the pan and set aside. Wipe out the pan with a paper towel. Return the pan to the stove.

4. Over medium heat, melt the butter in the pan. Whisk in the half-and–half, cheese, salt, and pepper until smooth and heated through. Add the pasta, a little at a time, tossing gently to coat.

5. Crumble the bacon and cut the shrimp into bite-size pieces. Add the bacon and shrimp to the pan and stir gently to mix. Serve immediately.

Recipe Substitutions
You can substitute scallops or chicken breast for the shrimp and this recipe will turn out just as good. Cook scallops until opaque, and chicken until no longer pink for a yummy alternative.

Italian Sausage, Taters, and Ketchup

Many kids in this age group like ketchup and may eat a lot of new foods as long as ketchup (or even barbecue sauce) is on their plate. This is one of those recipes where ketchup may be the ticket to an empty plate.

4 SERVINGS

1 pound Yukon gold potatoes

½ small yellow onion

1 pound sweet Italian sausage
(smoked sausage works too)

1 tablespoon extra-virgin olive oil

¼ teaspoon salt

⅛ teaspoon ground black pepper

2 tablespoons chopped fresh chives

2 tablespoons ketchup

1. Chop the potatoes, onions, and sausage into ½"
   pieces.

2. Heat the oil in a large skillet over medium-high heat.
   Add the sausage, potatoes, and onion. Cover, stirring
   often until the sausage is browned. Reduce heat to
   medium and cook for an additional 10–12 minutes or
   until the potatoes are cooked through. Sprinkle with the
   salt, pepper, and chives.

3. Serve immediately with ketchup for dipping.

English Muffin Pepperoni Pizza

These little pizzas can be topped with just about anything. Use cooked ground beef, drained chopped green chilies, and pepper jack cheese for Mexican pizzas; or chopped ham, drained pineapple tidbits, and Colby-jack cheese for Hawaiian pizzas. Your toddler will love helping you assemble these.

8 SERVINGS

4 English muffins, split

1 cup pizza sauce (store-bought or homemade—see the recipe in Chapter 7)

2 cups shredded mozzarella cheese

1 cup sliced pepperoni

1. Preheat oven to 400°F. Place the English muffin halves on a baking sheet and top each with pizza sauce and cheese. Layer the pepperoni over the cheese.

2. Bake for 5–8 minutes or until the pizzas are hot and the cheese is melted, bubbly, and beginning to brown. Serve immediately. Freeze for up to 2 weeks.

Sloppy Joe Pasta

Unlike traditional sloppy joes made with hamburger buns, this recipe incorporates pasta instead for an interesting twist on a classic recipe.

4 SERVINGS

1 pound lean ground beef
or ground chicken

½ yellow onion, chopped

½ **green bell pepper, diced**

1 cup water

1 cup tomato paste

2 tablespoons light brown sugar

¼ teaspoon paprika, or to taste

¼ teaspoon garlic powder

1 teaspoon kosher salt, or more to taste

¼ teaspoon ground black
pepper, or more to taste

1 cup whole-wheat pasta, cooked

⅓ cup shredded Cheddar cheese

1. Place the ground meat in a large skillet and brown over medium heat. After the meat is halfway cooked, add the onion and bell pepper. Continue cooking until the beef is browned and the onion is softened, about 10–12 minutes.

2. Add the water. Stir in the tomato paste, brown sugar, paprika, garlic powder, salt, and pepper.

3. Bring to a boil. Reduce heat, cover, and simmer for about 10 minutes, until the mixture is heated through and reaches the desired thickness.

4. Spoon the beef mixture over the pasta. Sprinkle with the cheese and serve.

Nuts Be Gone Trail Mix

This nutless trail mix is great to keep on hand to grab and go—or for serving nut-sensitive toddlers or their friends. Pack in advance using reusable snack cups and your toddler can enjoy this yummy, energizing snack all week.

10 SERVINGS

1 cup puffed rice cereal

1 cup pretzels

½ cup dried cranberries

¼ cup sunflower seeds

2 tablespoons dark chocolate chips

Combine all the ingredients in a large bowl. Store in an eco-friendly airtight container.

Cinnamon-Apple Pinwheels

Toddlers are amazed by the appearance of pinwheel sandwiches. Their interesting shape makes children eager to gobble them up. Make sure the apples are cooked until tender for easy chewing.

2 SERVINGS

1 small Gala or Granny Smith apple, peeled, cored, and sliced

⅛ teaspoon ground cinnamon

2 teaspoons honey

1 (8") whole-wheat flour tortilla

1. Spray a sauté pan with cooking spray and heat on medium-high. Sauté the apples until tender, about 5–7 minutes.

2. Mix the cooked apples with the cinnamon in a bowl. Set aside.

3. Spread the honey onto the tortilla. Evenly spread the apple mixture over the tortilla.

4. Roll up the tortilla tightly. Cut into 1" sections to make the pinwheels. Serve immediately.

Tofu Nuggets

These high-protein tofu nuggets are perfect for those who like a meatless option. Toddlers love dipping—so offer some healthy sauces with these, and they won't even notice that they're eating tofu!

12 SERVINGS

1 pound firm or extra-firm tofu

¼ cup whole-wheat flour

1 teaspoon garlic pepper

1. Preheat oven to 425°F. Grease a cookie sheet with extra-virgin olive oil.

2. Drain the tofu and cut into 24 rectangle-shaped bites.

3. Combine the flour and garlic pepper in a shallow bowl. Dredge each tofu piece in the flour mixture and place on the prepared cookie sheet.

4. Bake for 10 minutes or until golden brown. Serve warm.

Sweet Potato Cornbread Muffins with Maple Butter

These muffins will not last long in your house. They are a nice break from regular cornbread and are the perfect size snack for toddlers.

12 SERVINGS

1 cup unbleached all-purpose flour

⅔ cup yellow cornmeal

2 teaspoons baking powder

½ teaspoon salt

1 cup mashed sweet potato

¼ cup honey

¼ teaspoon baking soda

⅓ cup coconut oil or unsalted butter

1 cup whole milk

2 large eggs, slightly beaten

MAPLE BUTTER

½ stick unsalted butter, room temperature

1 tablespoon pure maple syrup

1. Preheat oven to 400°F. Lightly grease a 12-cup muffin pan with oil.

2. Add the flour, cornmeal, baking powder, and salt to a medium bowl. Stir until well combined.

3. Stir in the remaining muffin batter ingredients, being careful not to overmix.

4. Fill each muffin cup about halfway. Bake for about 20 minutes or until a toothpick inserted in the center of a muffin comes out clean.

5. Combine the butter and maple syrup in a bowl. Whip with an electric hand mixer until fluffy.

6. Break the warm muffins in half and spread with the maple butter to serve. Store remaining maple butter in an airtight container and refrigerate for up to 1 week or freeze for up to 1 month.

On the Move

Take a small lunch sack whenever you go out with your child and keep healthy snacks, like these sweet potato muffins, on hand. Packing a snack bag is not only helpful to have in a pinch (like in unforeseen weather that brings traffic to a halt for 2 hours), but it also eliminates the need to pop into a drive-through or convenience store and rely on less healthy alternatives.

Jumbo Stuffed Shells

Toddlers love eating these gigantic shells. This recipe is also good without sauce, if your toddler doesn't like sauce yet. Try it both ways.

12 SERVINGS

8 ounces whole-wheat jumbo shell pasta

1 pound baby spinach

12 ounces cream cheese or Ricotta

2 large egg yolks

½ cup grated Parmesan cheese

Pinch of ground nutmeg

⅛ teaspoon salt

⅛ teaspoon ground black pepper

1½ cups marinara sauce (store-bought or homemade—see the recipe in Chapter 4)

1. Preheat oven to 350°F. Bring a large pot of water to a boil. Cook the shells until al dente and remove, drain.

2. Steam the spinach in a double boiler until wilted, about 3–4 minutes.

3. Using a hand mixer, combine the cream cheese, egg yolks, Parmesan cheese, nutmeg, salt, and pepper. Fold the spinach into the mixture. Fill the shells with the cheese mixture.

4. Arrange the stuffed shells in a lightly greased 9" × 13" baking dish. Top with the marinara sauce. Bake for 30–45 minutes, until heated through. Refrigerate leftovers for up to 3 days.

Timesaver Tip

In order to make filling the shells easier, put the cheese and spinach mixture in a gallon-size plastic bag. Cut off the lower edge of the bag on a diagonal and squeeze the mixture into the shells. This technique can be used for filling cannelloni pasta or any stuffed pasta dish.

Lemon Shrimp

This is a family favorite that offers a healthy dose of omega-3 fatty acids. If your child doesn't prefer the taste of fish, try offering shrimp. Some toddlers will try shrimp just because they are small and cute!

8 SERVINGS

¼ cup extra-virgin olive oil

5–6 medium cloves garlic, crushed

2 pounds large domestic shrimp, peeled and deveined

3 tablespoons lemon juice

¼ cup chopped fresh flat-leaf parsley

1. In a large skillet, heat the olive oil on low. Add the garlic, and sauté for 2 minutes.

2. Add the shrimp. Sauté for about 5 minutes, until the shrimp are pink, turning often.

3. Add the lemon juice and parsley. Mix well.

4. Remove from heat and serve. Refrigerate leftovers for up to 3 days or freeze for up to 2 weeks.

Orange Chicken Stir-Fry

This stir-fry is very toddler friendly, with a sweeter sauce made of orange juice and honey.

8 SERVINGS
....

1 cup brown rice

1¾ cups chicken stock (store-bought or homemade—see the recipe in Chapter 4) or water

¾ cup orange juice

3 tablespoons tamari soy sauce (low-sodium)

1 tablespoon honey

1 tablespoon non-GMO cornstarch

1½ pounds boneless, skinless chicken breasts

Ground black pepper to taste

3 tablespoons extra-virgin olive oil or canola oil, divided

4 medium carrots, peeled and thinly sliced

1½ cups snow peas

1 large clove garlic, minced

2 green onions, chopped

1. Add the brown rice and chicken stock or water to a medium pot. Bring to a boil over medium-high heat. Reduce heat to low, cover, and simmer for 20 minutes. Remove from heat.

2. In a small bowl, mix together the orange juice, soy sauce, honey, and cornstarch. Set aside.

3. Cut the chicken into 1" cubes. Season with pepper.

4. In a medium skillet, heat the oil on medium-high. Cook the chicken for 5–7 minutes, until no longer pink.

5. Add the carrots, snow peas, garlic, and green onions. Sauté for 4–5 minutes, until crisp-tender.

6. Stir the orange juice mixture and pour it over the chicken and vegetables. Cook for 2–3 minutes, until hot. Add a few tablespoons of water if the sauce becomes too thick.

7. Serve the chicken and vegetables over the rice. Refrigerate for up to 3 days.

Pound Your Meat

Red meat and chicken can be difficult for your child to chew and swallow if it has been overcooked or if the chunks are too large. Therefore, cover the meat with plastic wrap and use a meat pounder (the back of a skillet or a rolling pin works too) to flatten the meat. Not only will it cook faster, but the meat will be a lot more tender and easier for your little one to chew.

Honey-Orange Carrot Jewels

Baby carrots are a great cooking timesaver because they are already peeled and trimmed. However, if you have regular carrots on hand, use them. The only difference is the appearance—your baby still benefits from the beta-carotene that carrots offer no matter which kind you use.

4–6 SERVINGS

2 cups baby carrots

4 cups water

2 tablespoons orange juice

1 tablespoon honey

1 tablespoon unsalted butter

⅛ teaspoon dried thyme

1. Rinse the carrots and place them in a medium saucepan with the water. Bring to a boil over high heat, then lower heat to medium and simmer for 5–8 minutes, until just tender.

2. Drain the carrots and return to the pan. Stir in the orange juice, honey, and butter. Cook over medium heat, stirring constantly until the sauce thickens and coats the carrots, about 2–4 minutes. Add the thyme and simmer for another minute. Cut into chewable pieces to serve. Refrigerate for up to 3 days or freeze for up to 2 weeks.

Know Your Carrots

Carrots are a great source of beta-carotene and vitamin A. A toddler-size serving of ¼ cup of regular carrots contains 3 g of carbohydrates and ¼ cup of baby carrots contains 5 g of carbohydrates. Studies have shown that beta-carotene is most effective when derived from natural foods and not from supplements, so don't worry about the carb count. Carrots are a carb expenditure that is well worth it.

Cheeseburger Soup

This hearty soup is loaded with the traditional flavors of an all-American cheeseburger. Make it for your toddler on a cold, wintry day to warm up after playing outside.

8 SERVINGS

¼ pound lean ground beef

2 tablespoons unsalted butter

¼ cup chopped yellow onion

¼ cup peeled and shredded carrot

2 tablespoons unbleached all-purpose flour

½ teaspoon Worcestershire sauce

1 tablespoon prepared yellow mustard

1 tablespoon ketchup

1¼ cups chicken stock (store-bought or homemade—see the recipe in Chapter 4)

1 cup whole milk

1 cup peeled and cubed russet potatoes

¾ cup shredded Cheddar cheese, plus extra for garnish

1 teaspoon dried parsley or 1 tablespoon chopped fresh flat-leaf parsley, for garnish

1. Brown the ground beef in a skillet, breaking it into tiny pieces as it cooks. Drain off excess fat and set aside.

2. Melt the butter in a large saucepan over medium-high heat. Add the onion and carrot. Cook until the onion is translucent, about 2 minutes.

3. Add the flour. Whisk in the Worcestershire sauce, mustard, and ketchup. Gradually add the chicken stock and milk, whisking constantly until thickened.

4. Add the beef and potatoes. Bring to a boil, then reduce heat to simmer. Cover and cook for 10–15 minutes, until the potatoes are tender. Stir in the cheese.

5. Garnish with a little shredded cheese and the parsley. Serve immediately. Refrigerate leftovers for up to 3 days.

Test Hot Foods, Especially Soups!

Always test the temperature of foods before giving it to your toddler. Soup, in particular, can be very hot and can cause significant burns. Therefore, make sure hot soups have cooled down enough to safely eat and always keep hot soups far enough away from children to avoid accidental spills and injury.

Smothered Tilapia

Tilapia is a mild white fish that's a good place for a toddler to start on her seafood adventures. In this recipe, it's smothered in a savory lemon sauce and baked to perfection. Serve over whole-wheat rice with a side of broccoli or green beans.

2–8 SERVINGS

4 tilapia fillets

¼ teaspoon salt, or to taste

⅛ teaspoon ground black pepper, or to taste

2 teaspoons dried dill

2 teaspoons dried parsley

2 lemons, juiced

1 tablespoon extra-virgin olive oil or unsalted butter

2 teaspoons unbleached all-purpose flour

½ teaspoon garlic powder

1. Preheat oven to 375°F.

2. Rinse the fish and pat dry. Season the back of the fish with some of the salt, pepper, dill, and parsley (in that order). Coat the bottom of a 9" × 13" baking dish with cooking spray. Place the fish seasoned side facing down. Season the front side with the remaining spices and herbs.

3. In a small bowl, combine the lemon juice and oil or butter. Whisk in the flour and garlic powder. Pour the sauce over the fish.

4. Bake for 20 minutes or until the fish flakes easily with a fork (do not turn the fish during baking). Serve immediately.

What's the White Stuff on My Fish?

Don't be afraid of the foamy white stuff that seeps out of the fish as it cooks. This is common to see on many types of fish, and it's a harmless protein that comes to the surface when the fish is cooked. If you think your toddler will object, simply wipe it off before serving.

Strawberry and Banana Muesli

This wonderful breakfast cereal is packed with fruit, dairy, and whole grains—and with so few ingredients, it's a snap to make. Pull up a chair and have some. This recipe makes enough for your baby and you too!

2 SERVINGS
. . . .
½ ripe banana

½ cup hulled strawberries

¼ cup rolled oats

1 cup whole milk

1. Chop the banana and strawberries into small pieces.

2. Combine the oats and milk in a small saucepan. Bring to a boil over medium-high heat and cook for about 30 seconds.

3. Add the fruit and mix well. Reduce heat to low. Cover, and simmer for 8–10 minutes, or until the oats are smooth and thick. Stir occasionally to prevent sticking and burning. Serve warm.

Holiday Turkey Breast

This recipe yields enough for a small crowd, with the potential for leftovers that can be frozen for later use. Instead of making a whole turkey for the holiday, this breast is another option. It still makes a nice presentation when sliced on a platter with leafy greens and cranberry garnish.

10 SERVINGS

1 tablespoon canola oil

⅓ cup honey

1 tablespoon dry mustard

1 (6-ounce) can frozen apple juice concentrate

2 teaspoons salt

1 teaspoon ground black pepper

1 clove garlic, sliced

4- to 5-pound turkey breast

1. Preheat oven to 325°F.

2. Combine the oil, honey, mustard, and apple juice concentrate in a small bowl. Stir well and set aside.

3. Rub the salt, pepper, and garlic over the entire turkey breast. Place the turkey on a rack in a roasting pan. Cover with foil and bake for 1 hour.

4. Uncover, add the honey-mustard glaze, and bake for an additional 1 hour.

5. Remove from oven and tent with foil. Let cool for 10 minutes before slicing and serving. Freeze for up to 2 weeks.

Spinach Pie in the Sky

It's no wonder Popeye the Sailor Man loved spinach. It provides folate, beta-carotene, and offers plenty of vitamin C to boot.

12 SERVINGS

1 tablespoon extra-virgin olive oil

¼ cup finely chopped yellow onion

1 (12-ounce) package frozen spinach, cooked and drained

1 cup shredded mozzarella cheese

½ cup grated Parmesan cheese

½ cup ricotta cheese

3 large eggs

1 cup whole milk

Ground black pepper to taste

1. Preheat oven to 350°F. Grease a 9" pie pan with oil.

2. Heat the oil in a small skillet on medium. Add the onion and sauté until transparent and fragrant, about 3–4 minutes.

3. In a medium bowl, combine the sautéed onion, cooked spinach, cheeses, eggs, milk, and pepper. Blend well.

4. Pour the mixture into the prepared pan. Bake for 30 minutes, until the top is golden brown. Serve immediately. Refrigerate for up to 3 days or freeze for up to 2 weeks.

Chunky Cucumber Topping

This is a great topping for crusty bread, fish, or chicken. Or, mix it with pasta—spaghetti, elbows, or shells—for a cool pasta meal on a warm night.

16 SERVINGS
················
4 Roma tomatoes, diced

1 cucumber, peeled and diced

¼ cup chopped red onion

1 tablespoon minced garlic

2 tablespoons extra-virgin olive oil

3 tablespoons red wine vinegar

Pinch of salt and ground black pepper

In a large mixing bowl, combine all the ingredients. Store in the refrigerator for up to 3 days or until ready to use.

What Is the "Extra" in Olive Oil?
Extra-virgin olive oil results from the first pressing of the olives. It's very versatile and works well for a variety of cooking methods. Virgin olive oil is from the second pressing. Pure olive oil is refined and filtered. Extra-light oil is highly refined and doesn't retain the rich olive flavor.

Magic Mango Coleslaw

The mango really gives this coleslaw a magical flavor from the tropics. For another edge on a classic side dish, substitute blueberries for the mango during their peak season to make Blueberry Coleslaw.

4 SERVINGS

2 cups shredded green or red cabbage or coleslaw mix

½ cup chopped mango

2 teaspoons chopped red onion

4 teaspoons balsamic vinegar

¼ cup honey

¼ cup mayonnaise

1. In a large mixing bowl, combine the cabbage or coleslaw, mango, and onion. Set aside.

2. In a small bowl, combine the vinegar, honey, and mayonnaise. Mix well to create a dressing.

3. Combine the dressing and coleslaw mixture. Toss well. Refrigerate leftovers for up to 3 days.

Compost It!
Toss your fresh kitchen scraps (no meat or oil) into a compost pile. You can purchase compost containers online that don't smell up your kitchen. Use the nutrient-rich compost in your home garden.

Cucumber Mint Lemonade

The fresh flavors of lemons and cucumbers unite in this blended drink. If your toddler hasn't quite accepted cucumbers yet, blending them in this drink ensures he's getting plenty of fiber and antioxidants.

4 SERVINGS

2 small cucumbers, peeled

1 cup freshly squeezed lemon juice

1 sprig fresh mint, stemmed

¼ cup honey, or more to taste

2 tablespoons granulated sugar, or more to taste

Combine all the ingredients in a blender and blend until smooth. Serve with ice. Refrigerate leftovers for up to 3 days.

Tricks for Juicing Lemons

Juicing lemons and limes without a juicer is not only possible but quite simple. There are a few tricks to extracting the most juice out of these citrus fruits. Trick #1: Warm lemons in the microwave for about 20–30 seconds. (Warm fruit juices flow more freely than cold juices.) Then, cut and squeeze out the juice by hand. Trick #2: Roll room-temperature fruit around on the counter with the palm of your hand. This will break up some of the membranes of the fruit. Cut and squeeze the lemon as hard as you can to extract the juice.

Quinoa Tabouli Salad

Tabouli is a Lebanese parsley salad traditionally made with bulgur or cracked wheat. This version uses quinoa, which is a pantry staple you may already have on hand. Because this salad uses a lot of fresh herbs, measurements are not a science—use your (or your toddler's) taste buds to determine if you should use more or less of any ingredient.

8 SERVINGS

2 cups water

1 cup uncooked quinoa, rinsed

1 small bunch fresh flat-leaf parsley

3 Roma tomatoes

3 green onions

1 sprig fresh mint

¼ cup extra-virgin olive oil

1 lemon, juiced

⅛ teaspoon ground black pepper

⅛ teaspoon salt

1. In a small saucepan, bring the water to a boil. Remove from heat. Add the quinoa. Cover and set aside until cool, about 20 minutes.

2. Meanwhile, finely chop the parsley, tomatoes, green onions, and mint.

3. In a large bowl, combine the chopped vegetables and herbs. Add the olive oil, lemon juice, pepper, and salt. Mix well. Toss with the quinoa. Serve immediately or refrigerate for up to 3 days.

Traditional Salsa

Using sweet Vidalia onions may be a safer bet for a young child than red onions for this salsa because they are very mild. Red onions, on the other hand, can be a bit strong for a toddler's taste buds, especially if it's the first introduction.

2½ CUPS

5 Roma tomatoes

½ medium green bell pepper, seeded

½ Vidalia or red onion

1 tablespoon lime juice

2 cloves garlic

¼ cup fresh cilantro

Add all the ingredients to a food processor. Pulse a few times until all the ingredients are finely chopped or pulse until a smooth consistency is reached if desired. Serve with tortilla or pita chips. Refrigerate for up to 1 week.

Sunflower Smoothie

Try this smoothie for toddlers going through a "picky" phase. It provides protein, calcium, and potassium, but the familiar flavors of banana, apple, and milk will appeal to many toddlers' taste buds.

4 SERVINGS

1 banana, frozen

¼ cup sunflower seed butter (such as Sunbutter)

½ cup apple juice

¾ cup whole milk or coconut milk

2 teaspoons honey

Combine all the ingredients in a blender. Blend until smooth. Serve immediately.

Leftover Smoothies
What do you do with leftover smoothies? Put your ice-pop molds to use for a healthy frozen treat.

Harvest Apple Risotto

News flash! You will not need to spend all day stirring, adding water, then stirring, then adding water, and stirring again to make risotto. This recipe is prepared by letting everything simmer beautifully in the pot until the liquid is absorbed, leaving you free to prepare turkey and a side of green beans to go with it.

4 SERVINGS

2 tablespoons extra-virgin olive oil

1 medium Gala apple, cored and sliced

1 teaspoon ground cinnamon, or to taste

1 cup Arborio rice

2 tablespoons cranberries (optional)

1½ cups chicken stock (store-bought or homemade—see the recipe in Chapter 4)

1 cup apple juice

3 tablespoons shredded Cheddar cheese

1. Heat the olive oil in a large skillet on medium-high heat. Add the apple and cinnamon. Cook for about 2 minutes, stirring until the apples start to become crisp.

2. Add the rice and cook for about 2 minutes, until the grains start to become shiny and translucent. Stir in the cranberries.

3. Add the chicken stock and apple juice. Reduce heat to low, cover, and simmer for 20 minutes.

4. Stir in the cheese and serve. Refrigerate for up to 3 days. Can be frozen for up to 2 weeks.

Cauliflower Dressed in Orange

Cauliflower has a mild taste and goes with pretty much anything—so it's perfect for toddler dishes. Dress up your cauliflower in a pretty orange dressing and serve with chopped salad to add a green element.

6 SERVINGS

1 head cauliflower

¼ cup full-fat plain yogurt

2 tablespoons prepared yellow mustard

1 teaspoon honey

½ cup shredded Cheddar cheese

1. Preheat oven to 350°F.

2. Cut the cauliflower into florets. Rinse under cold water to clean.

3. Steam the cauliflower in a double boiler until tender, about 5–7 minutes.

4. In a small bowl, mix together the yogurt, mustard, and honey. Toss the cauliflower in the sauce.

5. Transfer to 1½-quart casserole dish and sprinkle with the cheese. Bake, uncovered, for 20–25 minutes, or until the cheese is melted. Serve immediately.

Doctoring up Convenient Organic Foods
You can find a number of organic convenience foods at many supermarkets these days. When time is not on your side and you have to resort to purchasing some of these meals, doctor up the dish to pack in more nutrition and flavor. For example, add steamed diced Roma tomatoes to macaroni and cheese, add pineapples or bell peppers to a frozen cheese pizza, or top frozen waffles with fresh fruit.

Mango Pineapple Salsa

This fruity salsa can be used as a dip with tortilla and pita chips, or on top of fish or chicken.

4 CUPS

....

1 cup diced pineapple

1 cup diced mango

3 tablespoons finely chopped fresh cilantro

½ cup fresh corn kernels

¼ cup canned black beans, drained and rinsed

2 tablespoons lime juice

Pinch of salt

In a large bowl, combine the pineapple, mango, cilantro, corn, and black beans. Drizzle with the lime juice and salt. Mix well. Refrigerate until ready to serve or for up to 3 days.

Creamy Spinach Pita Pizza

Hmmm . . . what do you do with leftover Creamed Spinach? Use it to make a pizza! Or, what if you're out of pizza sauce? No worries, slather on the Creamed Spinach for a healthy alternative.

2 SERVINGS
• • • • • • • • • • • • • •

¼ cup Creamed Spinach (see the recipe in Chapter 4)

1 whole-grain pita bread

2 slices tomato

1 tablespoon grated Parmesan cheese

1. Preheat broiler. Spread the Creamed Spinach on top of the pita. Top with the tomato. Sprinkle with the Parmesan.

2. Broil for 2 minutes, watching closely to prevent burning. Cut into triangles. Serve.

Pizza Crust Ideas

When it comes to pizza crust, don't feel like you have to stick to the traditional method of preparing your own dough. Consider these alternative ideas to form the base of a pizza: pita bread, English muffin, prepared pizza crust, tortilla, or a whole-grain waffle. With a little imagination, a pizza party is always possible.

Chicken Enchiladas

Season the chicken with salt and pepper prior to adding it to the tortilla. If you have organic taco seasoning, you can also sprinkle a little on for extra flavor.

6 SERVINGS

1½ tablespoons unsalted butter

1½ tablespoons unbleached all-purpose flour

1 cup chicken stock (store-bought or homemade—see the recipe in Chapter 4)

1 cup sour cream

½ cup canned black beans, drained

2 cups cooked and shredded seasoned chicken

1 cup shredded Monterey jack cheese, divided

6 (6") whole-wheat flour tortillas

2 Roma tomatoes, diced

½ cup diced avocado

1. Preheat oven to 375°F. Lightly grease a 9" × 13" baking dish.

2. Melt the butter in a large saucepan over medium heat. Whisk in the flour for about 1 minute to create a roux. Whisk in the chicken stock, sour cream, and black beans. Cook until thickened, about 3–5 minutes. Reduce heat to low.

3. Meanwhile, assemble the enchiladas by placing a few tablespoons of chicken and cheese on the center of each tortilla (it saves time to assemble these in the baking dish). Roll up each tortilla and place seam-side down in the prepared baking dish.

4. Spoon the sour cream mixture and remaining cheese over the top of the enchiladas.

5. Bake for about 25–30 minutes or until bubbly. Remove from the oven.

6. Top the enchiladas with the tomatoes and avocado. Serve immediately.

Homemade Organic Taco Seasoning
In a small bowl, mix the following organic spices: 1 tablespoon chili powder; ¼ teaspoon each of onion powder, garlic powder, and dried oregano; 1 teaspoon each of kosher salt and ground black pepper; ½ teaspoon smoked paprika; and 1½ teaspoons ground cumin.

Pimento Boats

These are perfect for playdate snacks. Celery provides fiber, folate, and potassium and is great for stuffing with dips and spreads.

4 SERVINGS

4 stalks celery

4 ounces cream cheese

2 tablespoons sour cream

10 olives with pimento, chopped

Dash of paprika

1. Cut the celery stalks into 4" pieces.

2. In a small bowl, combine the cream cheese, sour cream, and olives with pimentos.

3. Spoon the cream cheese mixture into the celery and level off with a knife. Sprinkle lightly with paprika.

4. Cover, chill, and serve.

Broccoli Parmesan

Steaming is one of the best ways to cook broccoli, especially for toddlers. The stems retain a nice crunch while the florets are fluffy and tender. Some children love broccoli because they look like little trees—if yours does, try this variety.

4 SERVINGS

2 cups fresh broccoli florets

2 tablespoons extra-virgin olive oil

¼ cup grated Parmesan cheese

Kosher salt to taste

1. Steam the broccoli in a double boiler until tender, about 5–7 minutes.

2. Heat the oil in a large skillet on medium-high. Add the broccoli and sauté for 2 minutes. Toss the Parmesan with the broccoli until just melted. Season with salt to taste. Serve warm. Refrigerate leftovers for up to 3 days.

Caribbean Graham Snacks

These cute snacks taste like cheesecake (but crunchier!). If your toddler likes pineapple, give these a try.

8 SERVINGS

1 (8-ounce) package cream cheese

1 (8-ounce) can crushed pineapple, drained

2 teaspoons honey

4 whole graham crackers

¼ cup shredded coconut

1. Combine the cream cheese, pineapple, and honey in a medium bowl.

2. Break the graham crackers in half. Spoon 2 tablespoons of the cream cheese mixture onto each graham cracker and spread out evenly with a knife. Sprinkle lightly with the coconut.

3. Serve. Refrigerate the remaining cream cheese mixture to make additional snacks throughout the week.

Roasted Carrot Fries

If you want a nice alternative to French fries, try serving up a heap of these Roasted Carrot Fries instead. Your child will love the flavor while getting a nice dose of rich beta-carotene.

6 SERVINGS

3 large carrots, peeled and cut into ½" matchsticks

2 teaspoons extra-virgin olive oil

¼ teaspoon salt, or to taste

¼ teaspoon ground black pepper

1. Preheat oven to 450°F.

2. Arrange the carrots in a single layer on a baking sheet. Drizzle with the olive oil.

3. Sprinkle evenly with the salt and pepper. Using your hands, massage the oil and seasonings into the carrots.

4. Roast in the oven for 10–12 minutes, until crispy. Serve. Refrigerate leftovers for up to 3 days.

Zucchini Ships

This recipe makes a great appetizer for a party where toddlers are on the guest list. Arrange on a platter with Pimento Boats and Caribbean Graham Snacks (see the recipes in this chapter).

4 SERVINGS

1 zucchini

1 yellow summer squash, chopped

¼ chopped red onion

1 ripe mango, chopped

½ cup finely chopped fresh cilantro

2 tablespoons red wine vinegar

1 tablespoon extra-virgin olive oil

1. Slice the zucchini in half lengthwise to form 2 long boats. Scrape out the middle of the zucchini to form the hull of the boat.

2. Combine the squash, onion, mango, and cilantro. Toss with the red wine vinegar and olive oil until coated thoroughly. Fill the zucchini with the mixture. Slice and serve.

Zucchini Makes Great Bowls

Hollowed-out zucchinis make great vessels to hold different foods for a grand display or to simply eat food from. Fill the zucchini with any recipe that calls for zucchini and save yourself a few dishes to wash.

Grilled Pineapple

I first had grilled pineapple at a restaurant and ever since then I've been making it for the kids when I have pineapple on hand. You can use fresh or canned pineapple for this recipe. I prefer to use canned pineapple since I can never seem to cut the rings out of a fresh one, but if you can—go for it!

8 SERVINGS

1 (15-ounce) can pineapple slices

1 teaspoon ground cinnamon

1. Preheat grill on medium. Empty the pineapple with juice into a large bowl. Toss with the cinnamon.

2. Grill the pineapple slices until heated through, about 1–2 minutes per side. Serve warm. Refrigerate leftovers for up to 3 days.

Cilantro Lime Jasmine Rice

Serve this flavorful and fragrant rice with Lemon Shrimp (see the recipe in this chapter). To add a green element, try tossing in a few sweet peas.

8 SERVINGS

1 cup jasmine rice

2 cups water

2 teaspoons lime juice

1 tablespoon minced fresh cilantro

1. Add all the ingredients to a saucepan over high heat. Bring to a boil. Reduce heat to low and cover. Simmer for about 20 minutes, or until the water is absorbed.

2. Fluff with a fork. Serve immediately. Refrigerate leftovers for up to 3 days.

Zucchini Chips

These crispy breaded chips are great when dipped in Garlic Ranch Dressing (Chapter 7) or Marinara Sauce (Chapter 4). Panko is a Japanese-style bread crumb and is available organic. If you don't have panko, any bread crumbs will work. Try the Homemade Bread Crumbs recipe in Chapter 5.

2 SERVINGS
. . . .

⅓ cup panko bread crumbs

⅛ teaspoon kosher salt

⅛ teaspoon ground black pepper

1 medium zucchini

2 teaspoons extra-virgin olive oil

1. Preheat oven to 450°F. Grease a baking sheet with oil.

2. In a medium bowl, combine the bread crumbs, salt, and pepper.

3. Cut the zucchini into rounds, about ¼" thick. Coat the zucchini with the olive oil (don't be afraid to use your hands to make sure they are completely covered).

4. Coat both sides of each round with the bread crumb mixture. Use your hands to press it on if the coating isn't sticking.

5. Place each round in a single layer on the prepared baking sheet. Bake until crisp, about 30 minutes. Remove promptly. Serve immediately.

Sautéed Garlic and Dill Green Beans

Ever since I tried sautéing green beans instead of boiling them, I don't make them any other way. When I have cherry tomatoes that I need to use up, I cut them and half and throw them in the pot too. The green beans get eaten up either way!

4 SERVINGS
....

2 tablespoons extra-virgin olive oil

1 teaspoon dried dill

¼ teaspoon garlic powder

1 cup frozen Italian green beans (thawed)

⅛ teaspoon kosher salt, or to taste

In a small skillet over medium heat, sauté the olive oil with the dill and garlic powder until hot. Add the green beans. Sauté until the beans are tender, about 8–10 minutes. Season with the salt and serve warm.

Pineapple Gone Green Smoothie

Pineapple, orange, and apple rule in this snack, but it also includes a healthy serving of spinach. If you have yogurt on hand, feel free to add a little to the blender for a protein boost.

4 SERVINGS

1 cup spinach

2 cups cubed pineapple

1 orange, sectioned

2 Fuji apples, peeled, cored, and roughly chopped

1 tablespoon flax meal

2 cups orange juice

1. Place the spinach, pineapple, orange, apples, flax meal, and 1 cup orange juice in a high-powered blender. Blend until smooth.

2. Add the remaining orange juice and continue to blend to desired consistency. Serve immediately.

Flagging Winners

Have a system for flagging recipes your kids particularly like so you can quickly go back to them without scouring all your cookbooks to find them again. If your kids love this pineapple smoothie, and you noticed they drank it without complaint, use Post-its or flags to mark the page. Color coordinate according to which child liked it. Susie's favorite recipes could all be flagged with red Post-it tabs, while Johnny's could be all green. If you're reading the book electronically, use your eBook reader's "bookmark" or "highlight" option to capture favorites.

Raspberry Hot Chocolate

Adding puréed raspberries to a cup of hot chocolate is a great way to add a serving of fruit to this drink. Since raspberries and chocolate marry well, why not take advantage of the antioxidants the berries and cocoa offer?

4 SERVINGS

1 cup fresh raspberries

¼ cup unsweetened cocoa powder

½ cup turbinado sugar

Pinch of salt

2 cups whole milk

1½ teaspoons pure vanilla extract

1. Purée the raspberries in a blender. Set aside.

2. Add the cocoa, sugar, and salt to a medium saucepan. Turn the heat to medium, and whisk in the milk until smooth.

3. Stir in the raspberries and cook for about 5 minutes. Remove from heat. Stir in the vanilla. Serve warm.

Cocoa Has Health Benefits Too!
Studies show that cocoa may improve cholesterol levels and decrease blood pressure. Cocoa also contains flavonoids, an antioxidant commonly found in fruit and vegetables, that helps prevent heart disease.

Luscious Citrus Melonade

This juice drink is loaded with vitamin C and the honeydew provides a sweet, luscious flavor. Choose a honeydew with a waxy-looking rind with a surface that doesn't bounce back when pressed. Then, mix up this drink and head to the beach—with a pail and shovel for your toddler!

4 SERVINGS

2 cups cubed honeydew melon

1 cup orange juice

Blend all the ingredients in a blender for 30 seconds. Serve cold. Refrigerate for up to 3 days.

Vitamin C Powerhouse

With both oranges and honeydew in this juice, 1 serving provides 85 mg of vitamin C. The recommended daily allowance of vitamin C for kids ages 1–8 years old is 15–25 mg. This drink helps children meet—and exceed—those recommended levels. Vitamin C helps boost immune systems and protects against illness.

Strawberry Cantaloupe Dream

You can smell a cantaloupe even before cutting into it. The delicious fruity aroma will tempt kids on a weekend morning as they try to decide what they are hungry for. Once they smell the melon, they'll be craving this melon juice.

4 SERVINGS

½ cantaloupe, cubed

1 cup hulled strawberries

½ cup unsweetened coconut milk

Combine all the ingredients in a blender. Blend for 30 seconds. Serve immediately.

Ginger Pear Crumble

Look for firm, ripe pears to make this crumble. Bartletts have a sweet flavor that's great for baking. Pears are high in fiber and vitamin C.

10 SERVINGS

6 cups peeled, cored, and sliced Bartlett pears

2 tablespoons granulated sugar

2 tablespoons unbleached all-purpose flour

¼ teaspoon ground ginger

2 teaspoons pure vanilla extract

CRUMBLE TOPPING

½ cup unbleached all-purpose flour

¼ cup light brown sugar

½ teaspoon ground cinnamon

5 tablespoons cold unsalted butter, cut into chunks

1. Preheat oven to 375°F.

2. Combine the pears, sugar, flour, ginger, and vanilla in a large bowl. Mix well. Set aside.

3. Add the flour, brown sugar, cinnamon, and butter to a food processor. Pulse until the mixture is crumbly and the butter is incorporated.

4. Spread the pear mixture in an 8" × 8" or 9" × 9" baking dish. Sprinkle the flour mixture evenly over the top of the pears.

5. Bake for 40 minutes or until the crumble is light golden brown. Serve warm.

Choco-Nana Ice Cream

Frozen bananas make the best "ice cream"—with no dairy and sugar in sight! Your toddler won't miss the less-than-nutritious ice cream once she tastes this chocolaty delight.

8 SERVINGS
....

4 ripe bananas, frozen

2 tablespoons unsweetened cocoa powder

1. Blend the bananas and cocoatt powder in a blender until creamy, about 2–3 minutes. Scrape down the sides as necessary. If your bananas don't seem to budge in the blender, reposition them with a spoon a few times as necessary or allow them to thaw slightly before blending.

2. Transfer to a freezer-safe container. Freeze for 4–6 hours. Allow to soften slightly before serving. Freeze for up to 2 weeks.

> *Freezing Bananas*
> Freeze any bananas you won't get around to eating before they spoil. Just peel them and freeze whole. They don't brown outside of the peel if you freeze them immediately.

Cantaloupe Frozen Yogurt

When you make your own frozen yogurt, you can get really creative with ingredients. Cantaloupe is very tasty frozen alone, but when combined with yogurt It gets a standing ovation.

8 SERVINGS

· · · · · · · · · · · · · ·

1 cup diced cantaloupe

3 cups full-fat vanilla yogurt

1. Blend the cantaloupe and yogurt in a blender until creamy, about 3 minutes, scraping the sides as necessary.

2. Transfer the mixture to a freezer-safe container and freeze for at least 4 hours. Allow to soften on the counter for several minutes to reach a creamy consistency before serving. Freeze for up to 2 weeks.

CHAPTER 7
THE INDEPENDENT TODDLER—
2 TO 3 YEARS

Your child's development continues to charge along when she turns 2 years old. This is an exciting period—yet stressful at times, because there is a lot going on in key areas such as toilet training, transitioning from a baby crib to a bed, and dealing with tantrums. The good news is that mealtimes should get easier now that your child has plenty of experience feeding herself and is familiar with a variety of foods.

You may notice your child has a whole new perspective on eating and will comply during family mealtimes and happily eat her meal. By now, she should associate eating with hunger, but her preferences may change depending on what mood she's in on a particular day. With this in mind, go with her preferences while also offering other nutritious foods on her plate. If your child flip-flops often, don't make a huge deal out of it. Continue to be consistent with offering foods previously rejected. Eventually, your child may come around and decide she likes it—tomorrow!

Children between 2 and 3 years old are super active and will need nutritious foods during every meal to keep up with their high-energy requirements. You can still expect to provide your child with at least 1,000 calories per day, and if your child is participating in an outside activity in addition to the normal activities, consider providing 200 more additional calories. Offer snacks consisting of protein and unrefined carbohydrates, such as whole-wheat pasta, to sustain energy levels until the next meal.

SMART PORTIONS FOR YOUR TODDLER

The United States Department of Agriculture recommends that starting at 24 months children consume 1,000 calories per day, which includes the daily recommendation for each food group.

DAILY FOOD GROUP REQUIREMENTS	
Food Group	Amount
Fruit	1 cup
Vegetables	1 cup
Grains	3 ounces
Protein Foods	2 ounces
Dairy	2 cups

To get an idea of what this means, consider the following breakdown:

Breakfast
1 ounce grains
½ cup fruit
½ cup dairy

Morning Snack
½ ounce grains
½ cup fruit

Lunch
1 ounce grains
¼ cup vegetables
½ cup dairy

1 ounce protein

Afternoon Snack

¼ cup vegetables

½ cup dairy

Dinner

½ ounce grains

½ cup vegetables

½ cup dairy

1 ounce protein

Source: The United States Department of Agriculture, *www.choosemyplate.gov*.

You can switch around the types of foods however you like, as long as the basic portion requirements are met to ensure your toddler is getting enough calories per day.

IMPORTANT TIPS TO REMEMBER FOR THE INDEPENDENT TODDLER

- Switch to low-fat milk and offer plain water for your child to drink whenever she is thirsty.
- Bring your child along to help shop with you for foods and cook at home to encourage an active role in meal preparation.
- Take a few trips to pick-your-own farms to show your child where her food comes from.
- Transition your child from a highchair to a booster seat.
- Eat with your child at every meal and engage other family members at mealtime too.

Cinnamon Granola Crunch Cereal

This is my go-to recipe for making inexpensive cereal for my children. Granola can be eaten alone, as a topping, or with a bowl of milk for a nutritious breakfast. Even better, serve it with Fruit-Infused Milk (Chapter 5) to get a serving of fruit swimming in the mix. Unlike other cereals, this one takes a while to get soggy, so it's a win-win overall!

12 SERVINGS

½ cup packed light brown sugar

½ cup extra-virgin olive oil

½ cup honey

1 teaspoon ground cinnamon

1½ teaspoons pure vanilla extract

4 cups quick-cooking oats

1 cup shredded coconut

1. Preheat oven to 350°F.

2. Combine the brown sugar, oil, honey, cinnamon, and vanilla in a small saucepan over high heat. Bring to a boil. Remove from heat.

3. On a lightly greased baking sheet pan, combine the oats and coconut. Pour the brown sugar mixture over the top. Mix to coat well. Spread the mixture evenly.

4. Bake for 15–20 minutes, stirring occasionally. Let cool.

5. Store in an airtight container for up to 4 weeks. Serve with a bowl of milk or yogurt.

Cheddar Cheese Frittata

A frittata is similar to an omelet, but is served open-faced instead of folded over. The cheese is incorporated into the mixture and sprinkled on top for a beautiful grand finale. If your toddler loves eggs, you can easily incorporate veggies into this dish, too.

8 SERVINGS

4 large eggs

½ teaspoon dried parsley

⅛ teaspoon salt

⅛ teaspoon ground black pepper

1 cup shredded Cheddar cheese, divided

2 teaspoons extra-virgin olive oil

1. In a large bowl, whisk the eggs with the parsley, salt, and pepper. Stir in ½ cup cheese.

2. Heat a medium skillet on medium-high. Add the oil, tilting the pan so that it covers the bottom of the pan. Pour the egg mixture into the pan. Cook the frittata on medium-low heat, using a spatula to lift the edges occasionally so that the uncooked egg flows underneath.

3. When the frittata is firm on top, remove it from the pan, turn it, and slide it back into the pan (see sidebar).

4. Sprinkle the remaining cheese on top and cook for a few more minutes, until the cheese is melted and the frittata is cooked through. Serve immediately.

How to Flip a Frittata

To flip over the frittata, cover the skillet with a plate and turn the pan over so that the frittata falls onto the plate. Set the skillet back on the stove, and carefully slide the frittata off the plate and back into the pan.

Stuffed Strawberry French Toast

 T20

This is a broiled version of French toast to be made in the oven, using mascarpone cheese and strawberry preserves as the star players. If you don't have mascarpone cheese, cream cheese will work just fine.

8 SERVINGS
....
4 tablespoons melted
unsalted butter, divided

½ cup mascarpone cheese, divided

¼ cup strawberry preserves

8 slices cracked-wheat bread

2 large eggs

1 teaspoon pure vanilla extract

¼ teaspoon ground cinnamon

1. Preheat broiler. Spread 3 tablespoons of the melted butter in a 15" × 10" jellyroll pan.

2. In a small bowl, mix together ¼ cup of the mascarpone cheese and the preserves.

3. Spread the cheese mixture on 4 bread slices and top with the remaining slices. Cut the sandwiches in half to make triangles.

4. In a shallow dish, beat the remaining mascarpone cheese until fluffy. Add the remaining butter, the eggs, vanilla, and cinnamon; beat until smooth. Dip the sandwiches in the egg mixture, turning to coat. Place the coated sandwich triangles on the prepared jellyroll pan.

5. Broil 6" from the heat source for 4–5 minutes. Carefully turn the sandwiches and broil for 3–5 minutes longer, until golden brown and crunchy. Serve immediately.

Broiling Tip
Broiling requires a little attention to the oven to make sure the food doesn't burn. Place the food about 4–6" from the heated coils, and open the oven door slightly (needless to say, your toddler needs to be in another room when you do this!). Use the broiler pan that came with your oven, or a heavy-duty stainless steel pan that won't buckle under the high heat.

Best-Ever Pancakes

Pancakes are always a hit with young children. Serve these amazing pancakes on warmed plates along with turkey bacon and a cup of thirst-quenching water.

12 SERVINGS

1½ cups all-purpose flour

½ cup wheat germ or whole-wheat flour

3 teaspoons baking powder

¼ cup sugar

½ cup 2% milk

1 large egg

¼ cup water, or more as needed to thin

¼ cup canola oil

1. In a medium bowl, combine flour, wheat-germ, baking powder, sugar, milk, egg, and water. Stir until combined. If the batter is too thick, thin with a little extra water.

2. Beat egg white until stiff; fold into flour mixture.

3. Grease a skillet heated to medium with oil and cook pancakes until lightly golden, flipping once, until done. Transfer pancakes to a plate. Repeat with remaining batter.

4. To serve, cut a pancake into 1" sections. Spoon syrup over the top (try Spiced Peach Syrup or Blueberry Burst Syrup, both in this chapter). Refrigerate leftovers (separately) for up to 1 week.

How to Cook a Pancake

Use a ¼-cup measure to scoop out the batter, and pour onto a warmed, greased skillet (canola oil works the best). Make sure the skillet is not too hot or the pancakes will cook too fast and burn before the other side is cooked. Cook pancakes until the edges start to look dry and cooked and bubbles form on the surface, about 2–4 minutes. Carefully flip the pancakes and cook until the second side is light brown, 1–2 minutes longer.

Spiced Peach Syrup

Fruit syrups are super easy to make at home and can replace traditional pancake syrup purchased from the store. This syrup adds a vibrant peach flavor to any pancake or waffle.

6 SERVINGS
. . . .

¾ cup light brown sugar

¼ cup water

**½ (16-ounce) bag
frozen peaches**

¼ teaspoon ground cinnamon

⅛ teaspoon ground nutmeg

Combine the brown sugar, water, peaches, cinnamon, and nutmeg in a medium saucepan. Bring to a boil. Reduce heat and simmer on low. Store in refrigerator for up to 5 days.

Blueberry Burst Syrup

This easy recipe can be made in no time and keeps well in the refrigerator until you need it. Serve it with Breakfast Crepes (Chapter 6) or Belgian Waffle Wedges (Chapter 6) or as a filling for Homemade Toaster Pastries (Chapter 6).

6 SERVINGS
. . . .

**2 cups fresh blueberries,
rinsed and stemmed**

¼ cup sugar

1 cup water

1 tablespoon non-GMO cornstarch

Combine all ingredients in a small saucepan. Bring to a boil. Cook on medium-high heat for about 5 minutes, or until blueberries start to burst, stirring occasionally. Remove from heat. Sauce will thicken as it stands. Store in refrigerator for up to 5 days.

Zesty Breakfast Wrap

This recipe has everything your toddler needs for a wonderful breakfast. The eggs provide protein, the salsa offers a helpful serving of vitamin C and antioxidants, and the tortilla provides fiber. All you need to add is a sippy cup of milk!

2 SERVINGS

2 large eggs

1 tablespoon diced yellow onion

1 tablespoon diced green bell pepper

1 (6") whole-wheat flour tortilla

2 tablespoons mild salsa (store-bought or homemade—see the recipe in Chapter 6)

1. Spray a small skillet with nonstick cooking spray.

2. Beat the eggs in a small bowl with a fork. Add the onion and bell pepper.

3. Scramble the egg mixture in the pan.

4. Lay the tortilla flat and place the scrambled egg down the center. Top the egg with salsa. Roll up the tortilla, cut in half, and serve.

Chicken Goulash

The ground chicken in this recipe is great for toddlers because it's easy to eat. They'll also love the flavor-packed seasoning since it's not too spicy. For beef lovers, substitute lean ground beef for the chicken.

12 SERVINGS
. . . .

½ pound ground chicken

1 small yellow onion, chopped

2 cloves garlic, minced

1½ cups water

½ (15-ounce) can tomato sauce

½ (15-ounce) can diced tomatoes

2 teaspoons dried Italian seasoning

1 bay leaf

3 teaspoons tamari soy
sauce (low-sodium)

2 teaspoons kosher salt

2 teaspoons onion powder

2 teaspoons garlic powder

½ cup whole-wheat elbow macaroni

1. In a large pot, cook the ground chicken over medium-high heat until no pink remains, and crumble with a spoon.

2. Add the onion and garlic to the pot and sauté until the onion is translucent, about 5 minutes.

3. Add all the remaining ingredients. Cover and simmer on low heat for 20 minutes, stirring occasionally. Remove the bay leaf prior to serving. Refrigerate leftovers for up to 3 days.

Veggie and Hummus Platter

When the kids are playing around the house, it's nice to have a fresh veggie platter out so they can munch here and there. Playing builds up an appetite, so having fresh veggies available makes it easy for toddlers to grab and go.

4 SERVINGS
....

6 cucumber slices

6 red bell pepper strips

6 celery sticks

6 carrot sticks

½ cup hummus (store-bought or homemade—see the recipe in Chapter 5)

Arrange the vegetables on a round plate. Add the hummus to a small bowl and place in the center of the plate. Serve.

Homemade Bruschetta Topping

This recipe can be used to accompany pita chips, tortilla chips, crackers, French baguette slices, or crostini if you are looking to add a healthy vegetable component to those traditional snacks. Bring on the bruschetta!

16 SERVINGS

8 Roma tomatoes, diced

1½ teaspoons extra-virgin olive oil

1 tablespoon balsamic vinegar

⅓ cup finely chopped fresh basil

2 cloves garlic, minced

¼ teaspoon kosher salt

¼ teaspoon ground black pepper

¼ cup grated Parmesan cheese

Combine all the ingredients in a bowl. Refrigerate for up to 1 week.

Bruschetta Grilled Cheese

Spice up a basic grilled cheese sandwich by adding a little variety, and a serving of vegetables, in the middle.

2 SERVINGS

2 tablespoons unsalted butter, divided

2 slices whole-wheat bread

2 slices Cheddar cheese

2 tablespoons Homemade Bruschetta Topping (see the recipe in this chapter)

1. Generously butter one side of both slices of bread. Preheat a small skillet over medium heat.

2. Place a slice of bread butter-side down in the skillet. Top with the cheese and then the bruschetta. Place the other slice of bread butter-side up on top. Cook for 1–2 minutes, or until golden brown on the bottom. Use a spatula to flip the sandwich, and cook the other side for 1–2 minutes, or until golden brown.

3. Cut the sandwich into quarters. Serve immediately.

Basic Pizza Sauce

When I started paying more attention to food labels, I realized the main ingredient in store-bought pizza sauce was either tomato sauce or puréed tomatoes. Knowing I always at least kept tomato paste on hand, I came up with my own sauce and vowed to never buy store-bought pizza sauce again.

6 SERVINGS

6 ounces warm water

1 (6-ounce) can tomato paste

2 tablespoons honey

1 teaspoon garlic powder

½ teaspoon fennel seed

1 teaspoon onion powder

¼ teaspoon dried basil

¼ teaspoon dried oregano

¼ teaspoon ground black pepper

Pinch of kosher salt

In a small bowl, gradually combine the water with the tomato paste until it resembles a sauce. Stir in the spices. Refrigerate in an airtight container for up to 1 week or freeze for up to 1 month.

Freeze Your Pizza Sauce

Kids love pizza! Therefore, make a larger batch of pizza sauce ahead of time and use it to make French Bread Cheese Pizza (see the recipe in this chapter), Cheese Pizza-Dillas (Chapter 5), or even heat it up as a dip to serve with warm toasty bread.

French Bread Cheese Pizza

This recipe requires no kneading or rising. A prepared loaf of French bread is the answer when you need to prepare a meal in 15 minutes because that hungry toddler is whining at your feet! Save the remaining bread for another time. Bread freezes well, so put it in the freezer to make this recipe again. Serve with a small leafy green salad.

4 SERVINGS

1 cup pizza sauce, or more as needed (store-bought or homemade—see the recipe in this chapter)

4 thick slices French bread

1 cup shredded mozzarella cheese, or more if desired

1. Preheat oven to 400°F.

2. Generously spread the pizza sauce on top of the sliced bread. Top each slice with cheese.

3. Place the pizzas on a baking sheet and bake for 8 minutes, or until the cheese is melted.

4. Cut into small squares. Serve immediately. Freeze leftovers for up to 2 weeks.

5. To reheat, bake at 400°F for 3–5 minutes.

Endless Toppings
Use whatever veggies you have on hand, and of course your child's favorites, for pizza toppings. Chicken, crumbled beef, chopped peppers, and chunked pineapple are other great choices.

Garlic and Herb Corn

Corn made with garlic and herbs doesn't get many complaints from most toddlers. Serve with a lean protein and green salad.

4 SERVINGS

1 tablespoon extra-virgin olive oil

1 clove garlic, chopped

¼ teaspoon salt

1 cup frozen corn kernels

1 tablespoon fresh flat-leaf parsley

1. Heat a small skillet on medium-high heat and add the olive oil, garlic, and salt. Cook for about 1 minute or until fragrant, being careful not to burn.

2. Add the corn to the skillet and stir to coat with the oil mixture. Cook for about 5 minutes or until the corn is cooked through. Stir in the parsley.

3. Serve immediately. Refrigerate leftovers for up to 3 days.

Southern Shrimp and Grits

Toddlers enjoy this southern favorite, scaled back in heat to accommodate their palate. Serve with cooked spinach.

2 SERVINGS

6 large domestic shrimp, peeled, deveined

¼ teaspoon salt

⅛ teaspoon ground black pepper

½ cup grits

2 cups chicken stock (store-bought or homemade—see the recipe in Chapter 4)

2 tablespoons extra-virgin olive oil

1 clove garlic, minced

1 teaspoon lemon juice

1. Season the shrimp on both sides with salt and pepper. Set aside.

2. In a small saucepan, combine the grits and chicken stock. Bring to a boil, stirring constantly. Reduce heat, cover, and simmer on low until thickened, about 10–15 minutes.

3. Meanwhile, add the olive oil, garlic, and lemon juice to a medium sauté pan over medium heat. Add the seasoned shrimp. Cook until the shrimp are pink on both sides. Remove promptly.

4. Cut the shrimp into small chewable pieces.

5. Spoon the grits into a bowl. Top with the shrimp and drippings from the pan. Serve immediately. Refrigerate leftovers for up to 3 days.

Baby Cobb Salad

Toddlers get lots of healthy options in this cobb salad. Most likely they will use their fingers to pick off and eat their favorite ingredients first. Drizzle the dressing on top or serve as a dip for them to dunk the individual pieces in.

2 SERVINGS

½ cup coarsely chopped romaine lettuce

3 cherry tomatoes, quartered

½ hard-boiled egg, finely chopped

¼ ripe avocado, cut into small cubes

¼ cup diced smoked turkey breast

1 tablespoon Honey Mustard Dressing, or more as desired (see the recipe in this chapter)

Arrange the lettuce on small serving plates. In rows, arrange the tomatoes, egg, avocado, and turkey breast on top of the lettuce. Drizzle the dressing over the salad. Serve immediately.

Honey Mustard Dressing

This is a universal salad dressing that goes with every salad in this book and also makes a wonderful dip. To make more, just double or triple the recipe. You will never want to buy store-bought honey mustard dressing after making it yourself—it's so easy and doesn't contain any additives or preservatives.

½ CUP
....

½ cup mayonnaise

2 tablespoons honey

2 tablespoons prepared yellow mustard

4 teaspoons lemon juice

Combine all the ingredients in a small nonreactive bowl and whisk to combine. Store in the refrigerator for up to 1 week.

Southwest Potato Salad

If your baby loved the American Dream Potato Salad (Chapter 5), here is another power-packed potato salad with black beans for fiber and protein and lots of veggies.

8 SERVINGS

2 large Yukon gold potatoes, cut into small cubes

½ medium red onion, chopped

¼ cup minced green bell pepper

⅓ cup fresh corn kernels

¼ cup canned black beans, rinsed and drained

2 tablespoons minced fresh chives

⅓ cup mild salsa (store-bought or homemade—see the recipe in Chapter 6)

⅓ cup sour cream

¼ teaspoon salt, or to taste

⅛ teaspoon ground black pepper

1. Place the potatoes in a medium pot and add enough water to cover. Bring to a boil over high heat. Reduce heat to medium-low, cover, and simmer until just fork-tender, about 15 minutes. Drain and set aside to cool completely.

2. In a large bowl, mix the cooled potatoes with the remaining ingredients. Serve immediately or cover and chill for 1–2 hours and serve cold. Refrigerate leftovers for up to 3 days.

Garlic Ranch Dressing

Making homemade ranch dressing is more of an art than a science. I prefer to make my ranch dressing thin, but some people prefer a thicker dressing. Therefore, use the buttermilk (milk also does the trick) to thin the dressing until you're satisfied. This is another classic you can cross off your grocery list because you can make it yourself.

1¾ CUPS

2 cloves garlic, minced

1 cup mayonnaise

½ cup sour cream

2 tablespoons chopped fresh chives, or more to taste

1 teaspoon dried dill, or more to taste

Salt to taste

Ground black pepper to taste

¼ cup buttermilk, or more to taste

1. Combine all the ingredients in a small nonreactive bowl and whisk to combine.

2. Chill in a covered bowl in the refrigerator for at least 1 hour before serving for the flavors to develop. Store in the refrigerator for up to 4 days.

Homemade vs. Store-Bought: Homemade Wins!

There are a number of delicious dressings in the refrigerated section of your local supermarket, but homemade dressings taste so much better because they're fresh. You also save money making your own. Another advantage of homemade dressings is that you can customize them to your own taste by adding or subtracting ingredients.

Banana Cream Cheese Pinwheels

For best results, use a ripe yellow banana that hasn't browned yet. Bananas that are too ripe will be too mushy for the wrap. Any type of jam or preserves will work, so use your toddler's favorite.

3 SERVINGS

2 tablespoons cream cheese

2 teaspoons grape jam

1 (8") whole-wheat flour tortilla

1 firm ripe banana

1 teaspoon fresh lemon juice

1. Spread the cream cheese and jam on the tortilla.

2. Mash the banana. Coat with lemon juice to prevent from browning. Spread on top of the cream cheese.

3. Roll up the tortilla tightly. Cut into 1" diagonals to make the pinwheels. Serve. Refrigerate leftovers for up to 2 days.

Baked Teriyaki Wings

You will learn the art of basting by the time you are done with this recipe. It is important to baste these wings often, so that the color and flavors build. You'll end up with a thick and rich sauce. You have to babysit this dish a little, but the consistent basting pays off.

6 SERVINGS

1 tablespoon water

1 tablespoon non-GMO cornstarch

¼ cup tamari soy sauce (low-sodium)

¼ cup apple cider vinegar

¼ cup light brown sugar

1 clove garlic, minced

½ teaspoon ground ginger

6 whole chicken wings

1. Preheat oven to 425°F.

2. In a small saucepan over medium heat, combine the water and cornstarch. Stir until the cornstarch dissolves.

3. Reduce the heat to medium-low and add the soy sauce, vinegar, brown sugar, garlic, and ginger. Simmer the sauce for 10 minutes, stirring occasionally.

4. Meanwhile, arrange the wings in a 9" x 13" nonstick baking dish. Pour half of the sauce over the wings. Reserve the remaining sauce.

5. Bake for 45 minutes, turning the wings over halfway through the baking time and using the reserved sauce to baste the wings every 8 minutes. Serve immediately.

Super Crispy Chicken Fritters

I found out by accident that soaking chicken in salt water creates an amazing crunchy coating when frying chicken. I love to make a huge batch of these fritters about once a month because they freeze very well and are a great on-the-go snack for the kiddies.

8 SERVINGS

2 large boneless, skinless chicken breasts

¼ cup plus 1 tablespoon kosher salt

3 cups unbleached all-purpose flour

2 teaspoons ground black pepper

2 teaspoons dry mustard

1 teaspoon smoked paprika

Canola oil, for frying

1. Cut each chicken breast in half horizontally and then cut into vertical strips.

2. Fill a large bowl halfway with cold water and add ¼ cup kosher salt. Add the chicken and let soak for 20 minutes in the refrigerator.

3. Meanwhile, prepare the coating by combining the flour, 1 tablespoon kosher salt, pepper, mustard, and paprika. Mix well and set aside.

4. Fill a large pot ⅓ of the way with canola oil. Heat the oil on medium-high until hot. To check to see if the oil is hot enough, sprinkle a small dash of flour in the oil. If it sizzles, it's ready; if it just sits there with no sizzle, it's not hot enough.

5. Working in batches, take a few chicken strips and thoroughly coat with flour. Carefully drop each floured chicken strip into the hot oil. Cover and cook for 5–7 minutes, until light golden brown. Repeat this process until all the strips are cooked (you may only get 5–6 strips cooking at a time depending on how large the pot is, but don't overcrowd the pot).

6. Drain on paper towels. Serve immediately. Freeze leftovers for up to 2 weeks.

Honey Teriyaki Sauce

It's easy to make restaurant-style teriyaki chicken at home with this delicious sauce. Choose your favorite chicken nugget or fritter recipe from this book—for example, Surprise Chicken Nuggets (Chapter 5) or Crispy Honey Chicken Nuggets (Chapter 6). Combine them with this sauce in a pan over medium heat. Mix thoroughly and voila! Honey Teriyaki Chicken.

1 CUP
......

1 tablespoon water

1 tablespoon non-GMO cornstarch

¼ cup tamari soy sauce (low-sodium)

¼ cup apple cider vinegar

¼ cup light brown sugar

¼ cup honey

1 clove garlic, minced

½ teaspoon ground ginger

1. Combine water and cornstarch together to form a paste. Set aside.

2. In a small pot, add the remaining ingredients. Bring to a boil over medium-high heat. Stir in cornstarch mixture. Reduce heat to low and simmer for 10 minutes. Remove from heat. Refrigerate for up to 1 week or freeze for up to 1 month.

Bottle Your Sauces

Just like prepared sauces and dressings at the store, you can bottle your own. Simply take a recipe like this one, double or triple the batch, and store it in a bottle or jar in the refrigerator until ready to use. It saves a little time and can be used in other recipes calling for teriyaki sauce.

Cinnamon Watermelon Bowl

This dessert is a family favorite in the summer when watermelon is in season. It has exceptional flavor and provides a couple servings of fruit plus the antioxidants that cinnamon offers. This dessert can be very addictive for adults, but it's super healthy—go ahead and indulge!

4 SERVINGS

2 tablespoons canned unsweetened coconut milk, cold

1 teaspoon granulated sugar, or more to taste

1 cup cubed cold watermelon

½ banana, sliced

⅛ teaspoon ground cinnamon

1 tablespoon toasted coconut (optional)

1. Mix the coconut milk and sugar in a bowl. Set aside.

2. Combine the watermelon and banana in a small bowl. Drizzle with the coconut milk mixture and sprinkle with the cinnamon. Sprinkle the toasted coconut on top. Serve chilled.

Go Ahead, Serve a Wedge

Toddlers especially like watermelon wedges with cinnamon sprinkled on top. It's easy for them to hold and take bites out of.

Citrus Ginger Smoothie

The ginger in this chilled drink adds an unexpected twist to the citrus flavor. This drink is loaded with vitamin C for a healthy immune system.

4 SERVINGS
....

1 cup lemon juice

Pinch of ground ginger

1 cup orange juice

1 cup ice

Combine all the ingredients in a blender. Blend for 30 seconds. Serve immediately

Big Kid Taco Salad

Top this salad with chopped tomato and chunky salsa, sour cream, or more tortilla chips if desired.

6 SERVINGS
••••••••••••••

½ pound lean ground beef

1 tablespoon taco seasoning

1 tablespoon vegetable oil

½ small yellow onion, chopped

½ (16-ounce) can seasoned refried beans

2 cups chopped romaine lettuce

1½ cups tortilla chips

1 cup shredded Colby cheese

1. In a large skillet, cook the ground beef with the taco seasoning. Drain off the fat and transfer the beef to a large bowl.

2. In the same skillet, heat the oil over medium heat. Cook the onion until tender, stirring frequently, about 5–6 minutes. Stir in the refried beans and cook for 3–4 minutes, until hot. Combine the refried bean mixture with the beef and set aside.

3. Place the lettuce on plates and top with the tortilla chips.

4. Spoon the beef mixture over the tortilla chips and top with the cheese. Serve immediately.

Make Your Own Tortilla Chips
Choose corn or flour tortillas and cut each into 4 wedges using a pizza cutter. Arrange on a lightly greased baking sheet. Bake at 400°F for about 8–10 minutes, turning once. Sprinkle with salt and seasonings if desired.

Steak Quesadillas

Serve these tender quesadillas with sour cream and Homemade Guacamole (see the recipe in this chapter) on the side and a small bowl of fresh fruit.

6 SERVINGS

1½ cups sliced Slow Cooker Flank Steak (see the recipe in this chapter)

1 cup salsa (store-bought or homemade—see the recipe in Chapter 6)

1 (4-ounce) can diced green chilies, drained

6 (6") whole-wheat flour tortillas

2 cups shredded mozzarella cheese

2 teaspoons extra-virgin olive oil

1. Combine the steak with the salsa and green chilies in a medium bowl.

2. Place 3 tortillas on a work surface and divide the steak mixture among them. Top with the cheese and then the remaining tortillas.

3. Heat olive oil in a griddle or skillet over medium-high heat. Cook the quesadillas, pressing down on them with a spatula and turning once, until the tortillas begin to brown and the cheese melts, about 4–7 minutes. Cut into quarters and serve immediately.

Homemade Guacamole

Homemade guacamole is super easy to make and will make use of a lot of the veggies you may already have on hand, not to mention that it is cheaper than the store-bought alternative.

4 SERVINGS

3 avocados, coarsely mashed

1 lime, juiced

½ cup finely chopped Vidalia or red onion

2 tablespoons finely chopped fresh cilantro

2 Roma tomatoes, diced

1 clove garlic, minced

Combine all the ingredients in a bowl. Serve. Store in the refrigerator for up to 4 days.

Perfect Pairings

Serve guacamole with pita chips or tortilla chips, and whip up an extra batch to dress up meals like Steak Quesadillas (see the recipe in this chapter) or Chicken Enchiladas (see Chapter 6).

Hibachi Fried Rice

Leftover Coconut Teriyaki Shrimp (Chapter 5) adds a nice finishing touch to this fried rice dish. If you have any on hand, throw some in the skillet after the rice is added.

4 SERVINGS

2½ tablespoons canola oil

½ cup chopped white onion

½ cup button mushrooms, wiped clean

½ cup finely chopped napa cabbage

1½ cups cooked Jasmine rice, cold

⅓ cup frozen peas,
thawed and drained

⅛ teaspoon ground black
pepper, or to taste

⅛ teaspoon ground ginger

2 tablespoons tamari soy
sauce (low-sodium)

1 green onion, chopped

1. Heat the oil in a wok or heavy skillet. Sauté the onions, mushrooms, and cabbage until crisp-tender.

2. Add the rice, peas, pepper, ginger, and soy sauce. Stir until the rice mixture is evenly coated, about 2–3 minutes. Top with green onions. Serve as is or with a protein added. Refrigerate leftovers for up to 3 days.

Traveling Bean and Bacon Soup

This simple soup is great to take with you on the go, especially during the winter months when your child wants something warm to eat. Pour this hot soup into an insulated thermos for a meal that will still be hot a few hours later when he's hungry and cold at the playground.

4–6 SERVINGS

1 (8-ounce) package bacon

1 yellow onion, chopped

1 stalk celery, chopped

1 (14-ounce) can diced tomatoes, undrained

2 (15-ounce) cans pinto beans, drained

2 cups chicken stock (store-bought or homemade—see the recipe in Chapter 4)

Salt and ground black pepper to taste

1. In a large saucepan, cook the bacon until crisp. Transfer the bacon to paper towels to drain. Crumble, and set aside.

2. Drain off all but 2 tablespoons of the bacon drippings. Cook the onion and celery in the drippings (or 2 tablespoons olive oil, if preferred) over medium heat until tender, about 4 minutes. Add the remaining ingredients and bring to a simmer. Simmer for 10–12 minutes.

3. Use a potato masher to mash some of the beans. Add the reserved bacon, stir, and simmer for 5 minutes longer. Serve immediately, or pour into warmed insulated thermoses.

Creamy Coconut Soup

This is a great soup for coconut lovers. The toasted coconut enhances the appearance and provides a little crunch.

8 SERVINGS

¼ cup unsweetened coconut flakes

1 cup 2% milk

1 cup canned unsweetened coconut milk

1 cup water

⅓ cup light cream

⅛ teaspoon ground cinnamon

3 tablespoons granulated sugar

¼ teaspoon salt, or to taste

1. Preheat the oven to 325°F. Spread out the coconut flakes on a baking sheet.

2. In a medium saucepan over medium heat, bring the milk, coconut milk, water, and light cream to a boil.

3. While waiting for the soup to boil, place the coconut flakes in the oven. Toast for 5 minutes, or until they turn a light brown and are fragrant.

4. When the soup comes to a boil, stir in the cinnamon, sugar, and salt. Reduce the heat to medium-low, cover, and simmer for 5 minutes.

5. To serve, garnish the soup with the toasted coconut.

Aged Cheddar Cheese Soup

Choose good-quality aged Cheddar for a rich, creamy taste. This soup is so versatile you can add additional items such as cubed ham, broccoli, bacon, or potatoes—let your toddler choose!

8 SERVINGS

2 tablespoons unsalted butter

¼ cup chopped yellow onion

½ cup chopped celery

2 tablespoons unbleached all-purpose flour

¼ teaspoon dry mustard

½ tablespoon Worcestershire sauce

1 cup 2% milk

1½ cups chicken stock (store-bought or homemade—see the recipe in Chapter 4)

2 cups shredded Cheddar cheese

Salt and ground black pepper to taste

Pinch of paprika, for garnish

1. Melt the butter in a medium saucepan and sauté the onion and celery until tender, about 4 minutes. Add the flour, mustard, and Worcestershire and stir to combine.

2. Add the milk and chicken stock and bring to a boil. Cook for 1 minute, stirring constantly. Reduce heat to low, add the cheese, and stir occasionally just until the cheese is melted.

3. Add salt and pepper to taste. Garnish with a sprinkle of paprika. Serve immediately, or pour into insulated thermoses.

Vegetable Lasagna

This hearty veggie-packed lasagna surely meets all of your toddler's nutritional requirements—plus his taste requests. You could also add mashed tofu for an even bigger nutritional boost!

20 SERVINGS

1 tablespoon canola oil

2 cloves garlic, minced

½ red onion, chopped

2 heads broccoli, chopped

2 large carrots, peeled and diced

2 red bell peppers, chopped

2 small zucchini, chopped

2 large eggs

1 (15-ounce) container ricotta cheese

½ teaspoon salt

¾ cup grated Parmesan cheese, divided

4 cups marinara sauce (store-bought or homemade—see the recipe in Chapter 4)

½ pound lasagna noodles, uncooked

½ pound mozzarella cheese, sliced

3 tablespoons dried Italian seasoning

1. Preheat oven to 350°F. Lightly grease a 9" × 13" baking dish.

2. In a large saucepan, heat the oil on medium. Add the garlic and sauté for 2 minutes. Add the onion, broccoli, carrots, bell peppers, and zucchini, and cook until tender, about 8 minutes. Remove from heat and set aside.

3. In a large bowl, beat the eggs with the ricotta, salt, and ¼ cup Parmesan.

4. Ladle a small amount of marinara sauce into the bottom of the prepared baking dish. Layer the uncooked noodles, vegetable mixture, ricotta cheese mixture, and mozzarella cheese (in that order). Repeat layers to the top of the baking dish, ending with a layer of mozzarella. Sprinkle the top with the remaining ½ cup Parmesan and Italian seasoning.

5. Cover and bake for about 1 hour or until the noodles are tender. Allow to cool slightly before cutting. Serve warm. Leftovers can be frozen for up to 2 weeks.

Baked Coconut Shrimp

Although you can fry these shrimp, they come out just as good baked. Serve with Orzo Pilaf (Chapter 5) and steamed broccoli.

8 SERVINGS
• • • • • • • • • • • • •

1 cup unsweetened coconut flakes

2 large eggs

2 cups ice-cold water

2 cups rice flour

1 pound (about 24) large domestic shrimp, peeled, deveined, tails removed

1. Preheat oven to 450°F. Spray a baking sheet with non-stick cooking spray. Place the coconut flakes in a bowl.

2. In a medium bowl, beat the eggs and then stir in the ice-cold water.

3. Stir in the flour until the batter has a runny consistency similar to pancake batter. Add more flour or ice water if needed.

4. Coat each shrimp in the batter. Dip the shrimp into the coconut and place on the baking sheet.

5. Bake until golden brown on the bottom, about 4–5 minutes. Turn over and cook the other side until done, about 4–5 minutes. Serve immediately.

Turkey Roll-Ups

These roll-ups are another great on-the-go snack that travels well. Some toddlers love to peek inside the wrap and eat everything separately.

12 SERVINGS
. . . .

4 ounces vegetable cream cheese

4 (6") whole-wheat or sun-dried tomato tortillas

12 ounces sliced oven-roasted turkey

2 cups shredded red cabbage

1 cucumber, sliced

2 large carrots, peeled and shredded

Spread 2 tablespoons of the vegetable cream cheese on each tortilla. Top each with 3 ounces of the turkey, ½ cup shredded cabbage, slices of cucumber, and shredded carrot. Roll up the tortillas and slice each to make 3 smaller wraps. Refrigerate leftovers for up to 3 days.

Lemon Crunch Pasta

Make sure to cook your pasta al dente for this recipe, which means it will still have a nice bite. Overcooking the pasta (and also overheating leftovers) will result in a mushy mess that ends up sticking to your nice pan. If you don't have panko, any bread crumbs will work. Try the Homemade Bread Crumbs recipe in Chapter 5.

4 SERVINGS

3 tablespoons extra-virgin olive oil

3 tablespoons lemon juice

1 clove garlic, minced

1 teaspoon dried parsley

4 ounces whole-wheat spaghetti, cooked al dente

¼ cup panko bread crumbs

1. In a medium skillet, heat the oil, lemon juice, and garlic over medium heat. Sauté the garlic for about 2 minutes, being careful not to let it burn. Add the parsley.

2. Reduce heat to medium-low. Transfer the cooked spaghetti to the skillet and toss to coat with the sauce.

3. Remove from heat when thoroughly coated and warmed through. Top with the bread crumbs. Serve warm.

Pacific Cod Au Gratin

When choosing cod, stick with Pacific. Atlantic cod is considered a threatened species on the International Union for Conservation of Nature's "Red List."

4 SERVINGS
. . . .

¼ cup unsalted butter

3 tablespoons unbleached all-purpose flour

½ teaspoon dried dill

1 cup half-and-half

½ teaspoon ground nutmeg, or to taste

⅛ teaspoon ground black pepper, or to taste

1 teaspoon lemon juice

1 teaspoon salt

1 pound Pacific cod fillets (unthawed if frozen)

½ cup grated Cheddar cheese

1. Preheat oven to 375°F. Spray an 8" × 8" baking dish with nonstick cooking spray.

2. In a small saucepan, melt the butter over low heat. Add the flour and blend it into the melted butter, stirring constantly until it thickens and forms a roux, about 3–5 minutes. Stir in the dill.

3. Increase the heat to medium. Slowly add the cream, whisking until the mixture has thickened. Stir in the nutmeg, pepper, and lemon juice.

4. Rub the salt over the fish. Lay the fish fillets in the prepared baking dish.

5. Pour the white sauce over the fish. Sprinkle the cheese on top.

6. Bake for 25 minutes, or until the fish flakes with a fork. Serve immediately.

Baja Fish Tacos

Toddlers love the crunch that these tacos offer. You'll like the healthy fish and the nutrition the cabbage offers. Serve with Homemade Guacamole (see the recipe in this chapter).

8 SERVINGS

1 pound Pacific cod, cut into 2-ounce portions

3 limes, juiced, divided

¾ teaspoon salt, divided

½ cup light sour cream

½ cup mayonnaise

½ teaspoon dried oregano

½ teaspoon dried dill

¼ teaspoon ground cumin

8 corn tortillas

½ medium head green cabbage, finely shredded

½ medium head red cabbage, finely shredded

1. Preheat oven to 400°F. Grease a shallow 2-quart baking dish with canola oil.

2. Arrange the fish in the prepared dish. Sprinkle the fish with juice from 1 lime and ½ teaspoon salt. Cover with foil and bake for 10–15 minutes, until fish flakes with a fork. Remove from oven.

3. In a blender, combine ¼ teaspoon salt with the juice from the remaining 2 limes, the sour cream, mayonnaise, oregano, dill, and cumin to make the sauce for the tacos.

4. Heat the corn tortillas lightly in a skillet on the stovetop. Top each with a portion of cooked fish, drizzle with sauce, and place a handful of both types of shredded cabbage on top. Serve.

Slow Cooker Flank Steak

Pound the steak with a meat pounder and marinate overnight for the best flavor. Serve over mashed potatoes or rice with a side of sweet peas.

8 SERVINGS
....

¼ cup tamari soy sauce (low sodium)

2 teaspoons white vinegar

1 teaspoon onion powder

1 tablespoon honey

1 tablespoon light brown sugar

2 tablespoons extra-virgin olive oil

1 clove garlic, minced

1 pound flank steak

1. Mix together all the ingredients except the steak in a bowl.

2. Place the marinade and steak in a resealable plastic bag. Seal and place the bag on the bottom shelf of the refrigerator, on a plate. Marinate for several hours or overnight.

3. Place all the ingredients in a slow cooker and cook on high for 4 hours. Slice the meat and serve.

Rare Meat Is a No-No

Research has shown that rare meat products can carry bacteria, so children should only eat meat products that are cooked through. Anytime you cook meat, use a meat thermometer to check doneness before serving it to your little one.

Shepherd's Pie

Shepherd's pie is traditionally made with beef, but you can try using ground chicken or turkey (and chicken stock instead of beef) to change things up a bit. It's a hearty all-in-one meal that's perfect for a winter meal.

20 SERVINGS

3 large russet or Yukon gold potatoes, peeled and quartered

1 tablespoon extra-virgin olive oil

1 red onion, chopped

½ cup peeled and diced carrot

1½ pounds lean ground beef

¾ cup beef stock

¾ cup green peas

¾ cup fresh corn kernels

1 teaspoon Worcestershire sauce

1 teaspoon ketchup

1 teaspoon Dijon mustard

½ cup 2% milk

2 tablespoons unsalted butter

Salt and ground black pepper to taste

1. Preheat oven to 400°F. Bring a large pot of water to a boil over high heat. Add the potatoes.

2. Meanwhile, heat the oil on medium-high in a large skillet. Sauté the onion and carrot until tender. Add the ground beef and cook until brown, about 8–10 minutes. Drain off fat.

3. Add the beef stock, green peas, corn, Worcestershire, ketchup, and mustard to the skillet and cook for about 10 minutes, stirring occasionally.

4. Meanwhile, remove the potatoes from the boiling water when tender and drain. Mash with the milk and butter. Be careful not to make these potatoes too thin.

5. Add the meat mixture to a 9" × 13" pan, pressing it into the bottom of the pan evenly. Spread mashed potatoes on top of the meat. Use a fork to spread the potatoes in an even but pointy layer. There should be peaks of potatoes sticking up to get brown.

6. Bake for 30 minutes. Broil for 5 minutes at the end to crisp up the top. Serve immediately. Freeze for up to 2 weeks.

Creamy Dreamy Tortellini

I used spinach and cheese tortellini for this recipe but feel free to use whatever tortellini is available that your toddler would like. This dish is kind of like a soup, but it's so thick and creamy it deserves a small plate!

8 SERVINGS

12 ounces refrigerated tortellini

1 small yellow onion, chopped

½ cup chopped button or cremini mushrooms

1 tablespoon extra-virgin olive oil

1 clove garlic, minced

1 (15-ounce) can diced tomatoes

1 teaspoon kosher salt

¼ teaspoon ground black pepper

1½ tablespoons dried basil

2 cups half-and-half

2 tablespoons unbleached all-purpose flour

1 packed cup baby spinach

¼ cup grated Parmesan cheese

1. Bring a large pot of water to a boil. Add the tortellini. Cook for about 7 minutes. Drain and set aside.

2. Sauté the onion and mushrooms in the oil over medium heat until tender. Add the garlic, tomatoes, salt, pepper, and basil. Simmer for 10 minutes.

3. In a medium bowl, whisk together the half-and-half and flour. Pour the mixture into the pot with the tomato mixture. Add the spinach. Stir to combine. Cook on medium heat until heated through.

4. Add the tortellini. Stir to coat. Reduce heat to low. Simmer until thickened, about 5 minutes. Add the Parmesan. Serve warm.

Grilled Chicken Brochettes

Soak bamboo skewers in water for about 1 hour before using to help prevent burning or catching them on fire while grilling. Though you should put the food on the skewers, let your toddler help you make a pattern of vegetables as you assemble these—red, green, yellow, red, green, yellow, and so on.

10 SERVINGS

1 cup Honey Teriyaki Sauce (see the recipe in this chapter)

¼ cup Italian dressing

1 pound boneless, skinless chicken breasts, cut into 1" cubes

1 red bell pepper, cut into ½" squares

1 green bell pepper, cut into ½" squares

1 pineapple, cut into squares

1. Preheat grill on medium

2. Combine the teriyaki sauce and Italian dressing in a small bowl. Pour into a 9" × 13" glass baking dish. Add the chicken and toss to coat. Cover, and marinate overnight.

3. Thread the chicken, vegetables, and pineapple onto different skewers (for ease of cooking).

4. Grill until cooked through, about 8 minutes for pineapple and vegetables and about 12 minutes for chicken. Remove the chicken and vegetables from the skewers before serving to children.

Skewer-Soaking Tips

You can also soak the skewers in chicken stock for 1 hour, which will provide more flavor while cooking. Before cooking, coat the skewer lightly with canola oil, which can withstand the high heat of the grill.

Brazilian Coconut Rice

This rice has a mild coconut flavor and is extremely fragrant. The rice is first sautéed in a pan and then cooked until fluffy.

6 SERVINGS

1 tablespoon unsalted butter

1 cup long-grain white rice

2 shallots, chopped

2 cups canned unsweetened coconut milk

½ teaspoon salt

1. Melt the butter in a medium skillet over medium heat. Stir in the rice and shallots and cook for about 2 minutes, stirring frequently.

2. Add the coconut milk, sautéed rice, and salt to a medium pot. Bring to a boil. Reduce heat to a simmer, cover, and cook for 20 minutes or until the liquid is absorbed. Fluff and serve.

Orzo with Tofu in a Creamy Tomato Spinach Sauce

If your toddler likes tofu, this recipe may get two thumbs up! However, ½ cup diced chicken or beef can be substituted for the tofu. If using frozen spinach, thaw and drain before using in this recipe.

6 SERVINGS

¾ cup orzo pasta (or other very small pasta)

½ cup marinara sauce (store-bought or homemade—see the recipe in Chapter 4)

¼ cup silken tofu, drained

¼ cup chopped baby spinach

1. Cook the orzo according to the package directions. Drain and set aside.

2. In a food processor, combine the marinara sauce, tofu, and spinach. Process until smooth.

3. Transfer the sauce to a small saucepan. Heat through.

4. Stir the orzo into the sauce. Serve warm.

Barbecue Tofu and Quinoa

Quinoa and tofu combine for a protein-rich meal with a lot of flavor.

10 SERVINGS

1 pound firm or extra-firm tofu

1 cup button or cremini mushroom caps

¼ small yellow onion

1 large red bell pepper

1 tablespoon extra-virgin olive oil

½ cup barbecue sauce (see sidebar)

2 cups cooked quinoa

1. Cut the tofu into 1" cubes. Dice the mushrooms, onion, and red pepper.

2. Heat the olive oil in a medium skillet over high heat, then add the tofu. Cook 3 minutes, turning the tofu as it cooks.

3. Add the vegetables and cook for 5 minutes. Add the sauce and cook for 5 minutes.

4. Serve over the prepared quinoa.

Basic Barbecue Sauce

To make a simple, yet tasty, barbecue sauce, combine ¼ cup soy sauce, 2 tablespoons blackstrap molasses, 3 tablespoons honey, ½ teaspoon each garlic and onion powder, ¼ teaspoon ground black pepper, and ¼ cup ketchup.

Stir-Fried Noodles

Cut the linguine into shorter pieces before serving. Toddlers love to suck up the noodles! Serve with spinach or cut-up asparagus.

8 SERVINGS

2 quarts water

1 teaspoon salt

8 ounces linguine

2 teaspoons tamari soy sauce (low-sodium)

1 teaspoon honey

1 tablespoon red wine vinegar

2 tablespoons canola oil

2 cloves garlic, minced

1. Bring the water to a boil with the salt in a large pot. Add the linguine to the boiling water. Cook for 3–4 minutes, until al dente. Drain in a colander.

2. In a small bowl, stir together the soy sauce, honey, and red wine vinegar.

3. Heat the oil in a large skillet over medium-high heat. Add the garlic. Stir for a few seconds, then add the linguine.

4. Stir for 1 minute, then pour in the sauce. Stir-fry for 1–2 more minutes, until the noodles are heated through. Serve warm.

Cinnamon Pineapple Crumble

This delicious crumble can be served with or without a dollop of frozen yogurt or ice cream. You can also use canned pineapple chunks, but the slices are easier for toddlers to eat.

10 SERVINGS

2 (20-ounce) cans pineapple slices in juice

½ teaspoon pure vanilla extract

2 tablespoons unbleached all-purpose flour

CRUMBLE TOPPING

½ cup unbleached all-purpose flour

½ cup light brown sugar

½ teaspoon ground cinnamon

5 tablespoons cold unsalted butter, cut into chunks

1. Preheat oven to 375°F.

2. Set a fine-mesh strainer over a large bowl. Empty the pineapples and juice into the strainer. Pour the juice into a separate covered container and refrigerate to use for another recipe.

3. Empty the pineapple slices into the same bowl you used to collect the juice. Add the vanilla and 2 tablespoons flour. Mix well.

4. Add all the crumble ingredients to a food processor. Pulse until the butter is crumbled and incorporated into the mix. Note: You can also use a bowl and cut the butter into the flour mixture with a pastry blender by hand. That method is a lot more work but doable if you don't have a food processor.

5. Spoon the pineapple mixture into an ungreased 2-quart glass baking dish. Sprinkle the crumble mixture on top, spreading it out evenly.

6. Bake for 45 minutes or until the topping is a light golden brown. Serve warm.

Chicken Wraps

Cream cheese is the "glue" that holds this wrap together. It's very simple to flavor the cream cheese for a nice twist. Have your child stir the cream cheese mixture herself!

4 SERVINGS

3 ounces cream cheese,
at room temperature

1 tablespoon mayonnaise

1 tablespoon lemon juice

¼ teaspoon salt

Ground black pepper to taste

2 (8") whole-wheat flour tortillas

2 cups sliced or cubed cooked chicken

½ cup thinly sliced red onion

1 cup baby spinach

1. Mix together the cream cheese, mayonnaise, lemon juice, salt, and pepper in a small bowl

2. Place the tortillas on a clean work surface. Spread half the cream cheese mixture on the upper third of each tortilla, about ½" from the edge. Place half the chicken on the lower third of each tortilla. Top each with the onions and spinach.

3. Roll up each wrap: Starting from the bottom, fold the tortilla over the filling and roll upward, compressing slightly to form a firm roll. Press at the top to "seal" the wrap closed with the cream cheese mixture. Cut the sandwich in half and wrap in plastic film. Refrigerate for up to 3 days.

BLTA Wrap

Bacon, lettuce, tomato . . . and avocado are the star players in this tasty wrap. The avocado adds some healthy fats that your toddler needs as he grows. Drizzle lime juice over the avocado to keep it from browning.

4 SERVINGS

3 ounces cream cheese, at room temperature

2 tablespoons mayonnaise

¼ teaspoon salt

Ground black pepper to taste

2 (8") whole-wheat flour tortillas, at room temperature

6 slices smoked bacon, cooked

¼ cup diced avocado

¼ cup seeded and diced ripe tomato

1 cup chopped romaine lettuce hearts

1. Mix together the cream cheese, mayonnaise, salt, and pepper in a small bowl (or use a food processor to blend until smooth).

2. Place the tortillas on a work surface. Spread half the cream cheese mixture on the upper third of each tortilla, about ½" from the edge. Place half the bacon on the lower third of each tortilla. Top each with the avocado, tomato, and lettuce.

3. Roll up each wrap: Starting from the bottom, fold the tortilla over the filling and roll upward, compressing slightly to form a firm roll. Press at the top to "seal" the wrap closed with the cream cheese mixture. Cut the sandwich in half and wrap in plastic film. Refrigerate leftovers for up to 3 days.

Mexican Burger Dogs

These dogs are similar to a taco, but prepared in a hot dog bun instead of a taco shell. The soft buns make it easier for little mouths to chew, and they are a great option if your toddler doesn't like the crunch of a hard taco shell.

8 SERVINGS

1 pound lean ground beef
or ground chicken

½ small yellow onion, chopped

¼ cup frozen corn kernels

½ teaspoon salt

⅓ cup salsa (store-bought
or homemade—see the
recipe in Chapter 6)

8 whole-wheat hot dog buns

¼ cup diced avocado

½ cup shredded Cheddar cheese

1. Add the ground meat to a large skillet over medium-high heat. Add the onion, corn, and salt. Mix well. Cook until the meat is no longer pink. Drain off fat.

2. Add the salsa to the skillet and mix well. Cook for about 2 minutes, until heated through.

3. Scoop a couple tablespoons of the hot meat mixture into each hot dog bun. Top with the avocado and cheese. Serve immediately.

Monkey Muffins

The sweet smell of bananas will tempt tiny taste buds! Serve with a ½ hard-boiled egg and a sippy cup of milk with a small slice of a tasty muffin for an afternoon snack.

12 SERVINGS

1½ cups all-purpose flour

2 tablespoons baking powder

½ teaspoon salt

3 ripe bananas

¾ cup light brown sugar

1 egg

⅓ cup butter, melted

1. Combine flour, baking powder, and salt in a bowl. Set aside.

2. In a separate bowl, mash the bananas with a fork. Add the sugar, butter, and egg, and mix together with the fork until thoroughly combined.

3. Add wet ingredients to dry ingredients. Mix until just combined; be careful not to overmix.

4. Divide the batter among 12 standard muffin cups. Bake for 20–25 minutes or until muffins are golden brown. Freeze for up to 2 weeks.

Strawberry Banana Surprise

Use frozen fruit to make smoothies rich, creamy, and extra cold. Peel bananas and freeze them whole (in a freezer bag) for this delicious breakfast or snack.

4 SERVINGS
....

2 bananas, frozen

1 cup fresh or frozen sliced strawberries

1 cup low-fat vanilla or strawberry yogurt

1½ cups orange juice

½ cup organic cereal O's

1. Place the bananas, strawberries, yogurt, and orange juice in a blender and blend until smooth.

2. Pour into glasses and top with a spoonful of cereal O's for a surprise garnish. Serve immediately.

Mango Raspberry Salsa

Toddlers can never have too many salsa options for dipping and dunking tortilla chips, veggies, crackers, and pita bread. This fruity salsa features raspberries as the starlet.

2½ CUPS

1 cup chopped mango

1 cup fresh raspberries

¼ cup minced fresh cilantro

⅓ cup chopped Vidalia onion

3 tablespoons lime juice

½ teaspoon granulated sugar

Combine all the ingredients in a bowl. Chill for at least 30 minutes before serving. Refrigerate for up to 5 days.

Make the Most of the Food Processor

For recipes that require a lot of dicing and chopping, put your food processor to work. Do the bare minimum (washing and peeling, then cutting anything too big to fit in the container), then throw everything in the food processor and pulse away!

Pineapple Peach Pick Me Up

Nothing starts a toddler's engine better in the morning than a glass full of manganese. This trace mineral, contained in high doses in pineapple, is an essential part of energy production.

4 SERVINGS
. . . .

1 (15-ounce) can pineapple chunks in juice

1 peach, pitted

¼ cup apple juice

Combine all the ingredients in a blender. Blend for 30 seconds. Serve immediately.

Cucumber Melon Zinger

This fresh zinger will add an ounce of happiness to cranky toddlers. The zing of cucumber mixed with the sweet taste from the melons and apple juice is enough to give them a smile—for a while.

2 SERVINGS

1 cucumber, peeled

½ honeydew melon, seeded and cut into large chunks

1 cup apple juice

Combine all ingredients in a blender. Blend for 30 seconds. Serve chilled or over ice.

Water-Soluble Vitamin C

Essential vitamins are the vitamins we can only obtain through our diet. Fat-soluble vitamins, such as vitamins A, D, E, and K, can be stored in our bodies for a long period of time, but water-soluble vitamins, like vitamin C, cannot be stored and need to be eaten daily. One cup of cantaloupe has over 100 percent of the daily requirement for vitamin C. Drinking fresh juices with ingredients such as cantaloupe and cucumbers can help kids meet their daily need for vitamin C. Serving these vitamin C–rich juices first thing in the morning can put your mind at ease.

Banana Bonanza Quesadillas with Raspberry Sauce

When your child wants something sweet, this healthy dessert will certainly satisfy his sweet tooth while providing a healthy serving of whole grain, potassium, and antioxidants.

4 SERVINGS

¼ cup cream cheese

1 tablespoon honey

1 banana

1 tablespoon unsalted butter

2 (8") whole-wheat flour tortillas

¼ teaspoon ground cinnamon

RASPBERRY SAUCE

¾ cup frozen raspberries, thawed

1½ tablespoons lemon juice

1 tablespoon granulated sugar

1. Make the raspberry sauce by combining all ingredients in a blender. Set in the refrigerator until ready to use.

2. Combine the cream cheese and honey in a small bowl. Set aside. Cut the banana into slices.

3. Generously butter one side of each tortilla. Spread the cream cheese mixture on the other side.

4. Heat a flat skillet over medium heat. Place a tortilla butter-side down on the skillet. Quickly arrange the banana slices in the center, 1" from the edge. Sprinkle with the cinnamon. Place the other tortilla butter-side up on top of the bananas.

5. Cook the quesadilla until the bottom is lightly golden, about 3–4 minutes. Carefully flip the quesadilla using a large spatula. Cook until lightly golden on the other side, about 3–4 minutes.

6. Cut into quarters with a pizza cutter. Drizzle with the raspberry sauce. Serve.

Moist Oatmeal Cranberry Cookies

This ingredient list seems long, but these are no more difficult to make than other cookies. They come out super moist, and they're addictive! It is very easy to eat several at once, so make 12 cookies for starters, and freeze the remaining dough for later. Don't forget to save some for your children!

24 SERVINGS

1½ cups unbleached all-purpose flour

2 cups quick-cooking oats

½ teaspoon salt

¾ teaspoon ground cinnamon

1 teaspoon baking soda

1 stick unsalted butter

½ cup turbinado sugar

½ cup light brown sugar

2 teaspoons pure vanilla extract

1 tablespoon honey

1 tablespoon molasses

2 large eggs

½ cup dried cranberries

1. Preheat oven to 350°F. Line a cookie sheet with a Silpat liner or parchment paper.

2. Combine the flour, oats, salt, cinnamon, and baking soda in a medium mixing bowl. Set aside.

3. Cream the butter and sugars together in a stand mixer with a paddle attachment or use a hand mixer. Beat on medium speed until light and fluffy. Add the vanilla, honey, and molasses.

4. Beat the eggs into the mixture, one at a time, until well blended. Scrape the mixture from the sides of the bowl. Add the flour mixture, gradually, until well combined. Fold in the cranberries.

5. Scoop the cookie dough into 2" balls with a melon baller. Place 2" apart on the prepared baking sheet.

6. Bake for about 10–12 minutes. Remove from the oven and let cool. Freeze remaining dough for up to 8 weeks.

What Is a Silpat Liner?

Silpat liners are flexible, silicone, nonstick baking sheets that save time and hassle with cleanup. They are a must-have if you love to bake because nothing sticks to them and your pans won't get that yucky burnt look.

Balsamic Strawberry Yogurt Pops

Balsamic vinegar and strawberries? Isn't that an odd combination? I had that question after hearing so many people rave about the amazing taste of them paired together. Since I always have balsamic vinegar on hand, one day I figured I'd try it out and see what the kids thought of it. This recipe has since become a winner!

4 SERVINGS

2 cups chopped fresh strawberries

2 tablespoons turbinado sugar

½ teaspoon pure vanilla extract

1 tablespoon balsamic vinegar

1 cup plain or vanilla Greek yogurt

1. Combine the strawberries, sugar, vanilla, and vinegar in a medium bowl. Cover and refrigerate for 30 minutes to allow the flavors to develop.

2. Spoon yogurt into the popsicle molds to about ⅓ full. Add alternating layers of the strawberry mixture and remaining yogurt, ending with a layer of strawberry mixture on top.

3. Freeze for 24 hours. To remove the popsicles from the mold, run warm water over them, and they should slide right out.

APPENDIX

RESOURCES

ORGANIC INFORMATION

The National Organic Program
www.ams.usda.gov/NOP

The Organic Trade Association
www.ota.com

The Organic Trade Association's Organic Report
www.organicitsworthit.org

The Environmental Working Group
www.ewg.org

Organic Consumers Association
www.organicconsumers.org

FARMERS' MARKETS AND ORGANIC STORES

Organic.org
www.organic.org

The Alternative Farming Systems Information Center
http://afsic.nal.usda.gov

National Sustainable Agriculture Information Service
https://attra.ncat.org

PickYourOwn.org
www.pickyourown.org

NUTRITION AND MEDICAL INFORMATION

USDA Dietary Guidelines for Americans
www.choosemyplate.gov

American Academy of Pediatrics
www.aap.org

Academy of Nutrition and Dietetics
www.eatright.org

Food Allergy Research & Education
www.foodallergy.org

HealthyChildren.org
www.healthychildren.org

"The Chemical Age Dawns in Agriculture," by Bill Ganzel
www.livinghistoryfarm.org/farminginthe40s/pests_01.html

MORE HOMEMADE BABY FOOD RECIPES AND TODDLER MEALS

Simply Baby Food Recipes
www.simplybabyfoodrecipes.net

INDEX

· · · · · · · · · ·

Tamika L. Gardner is the author of *201 Organic Baby Purées*, a cookbook full of nutritious purée recipes for infants 6 to 9 months old. She is also the founder of *www.SimplyBabyFoodRecipes.net*.

As a thrifty mom who exclusively breastfed her children, purchasing processed food seemed both expensive and unhealthy. After seeking advice from her grandmother, who always mashed up fresh food for her six children, Tamika began to purée food for her children. With more than eight years of experience as a "baby chef," Tamika continues on her journey, and with her growing family, lives an abundant, healthy life free of illness and disease. She believes that a diet rich in fruit and vegetables is the cornerstone to achieving great health, and aims to inspire parents to nurture healthy children for generations to come.